FOR ORGANS, PIANOS & ELECTRONIC KEYBOARDS

280

CLASSICAL
A Night At The Sy[mphony]

GW01079994

ISBN 0-7935-1626-9

Hal Leonard Publishing Corporation
7777 West Bluemound Road P.O. Box 13819 Milwaukee, WI 53213

E-Z Play ® TODAY Music Notation © 1975 HAL LEONARD PUBLISHING CORPORATION
Copyright © 1992 by HAL LEONARD PUBLISHING CORPORATION
International Copyright Secured   All Rights Reserved

For all works contained herein:
Unauthorized copying, arranging, adapting, recording or public performance is an infringement of copyright.
Infringers are liable under the law.

E-Z PLAY and EASY ELECTRONIC KEYBOARD MUSIC are registered trademarks of HAL LEONARD PUBLISHING CORPORATION.

Contents
Classical Hits - A Night At The Symphony

4	Academic Festival Overture	*Johannes Brahms*	
8	Also Sprach Zarathustra	*Richard Strauss*	
10	Capriccio Italien	*Peter Ilyich Tchaikovsky*	
12	Eine Kleine Nachtmusik (First Movement Theme)	*Wolfgang Amadeus Mozart*	
14	Great Gate Of Kiev (From PICTURES AT AN EXHIBITION)	*Modeste Mussorgsky*	
15	In The Hall Of The Mountain King (From PEER GYNT SUITE)	*Edvard Grieg*	
18	March (From TANNHAUSER)	*Richard Wagner*	
20	Marche Slav	*Peter Ilyich Tchaikovsky*	
22	Moldau, The (From MA VLAST)	*Bedrich Smetana*	
28	Piano Concerto in A minor (First Movement Theme)	*Edvard Grieg*	
25	Piano Concerto in C Major (Second Movement Theme)	*Wolfgang Amadeus Mozart*	
30	Piano Concerto No. 1 in B-flat minor, Op. 23 (First Movement Theme)	*Peter Ilyich Tchaikovsky*	
34	Piano Concerto No. 5 ("Emperor") (First Movement)	*Ludwig van Beethoven*	
32	Poet And Peasant Overture	*Franz von Suppe*	
36	Ride Of The Valkyries (From DIE WALKURE)	*Richard Wagner*	
35	Surprise Symphony (Second Movement Theme)	*Franz Joseph Haydn*	
38	Symphony No. 1 (Fourth Movement Chorale)	*Johannes Brahms*	
40	Symphony No. 3 ("Eroica") (First Movement Theme)	*Ludwig van Beethoven*	
42	Symphony No. 4 (Third Movement Theme)	*Johannes Brahms*	
52	Symphony No. 5 (First Movement Theme)	*Ludwig van Beethoven*	
44	Symphony No. 6 ("Pathetique") (First Movement Theme)	*Peter Ilyich Tchaikovsky*	
46	Symphony No. 6 ("Pastoral") (First Movement Theme)	*Ludwig van Beethoven*	
48	Symphony No. 7 (Second Movement Theme)	*Ludwig van Beethoven*	
50	Symphony No. 8 ("Unfinished") (First Movement Theme)	*Franz Schubert*	
55	Symphony No. 9 ("From The New World") (Second Movement, "Largo")	*Anton Dvorak*	
58	Symphony No. 9 (Fourth Movement Theme, "Ode To Joy")	*Ludwig van Beethoven*	
61	Symphony No. 40 (First Movement Theme)	*Wolfgang Amadeus Mozart*	
64	Violin Concerto (First Movement Theme)	*Felix Mendelssohn*	
68	William Tell Overture (Closing Theme)	*Gioachino Rossini*	
72	REGISTRATION GUIDE		

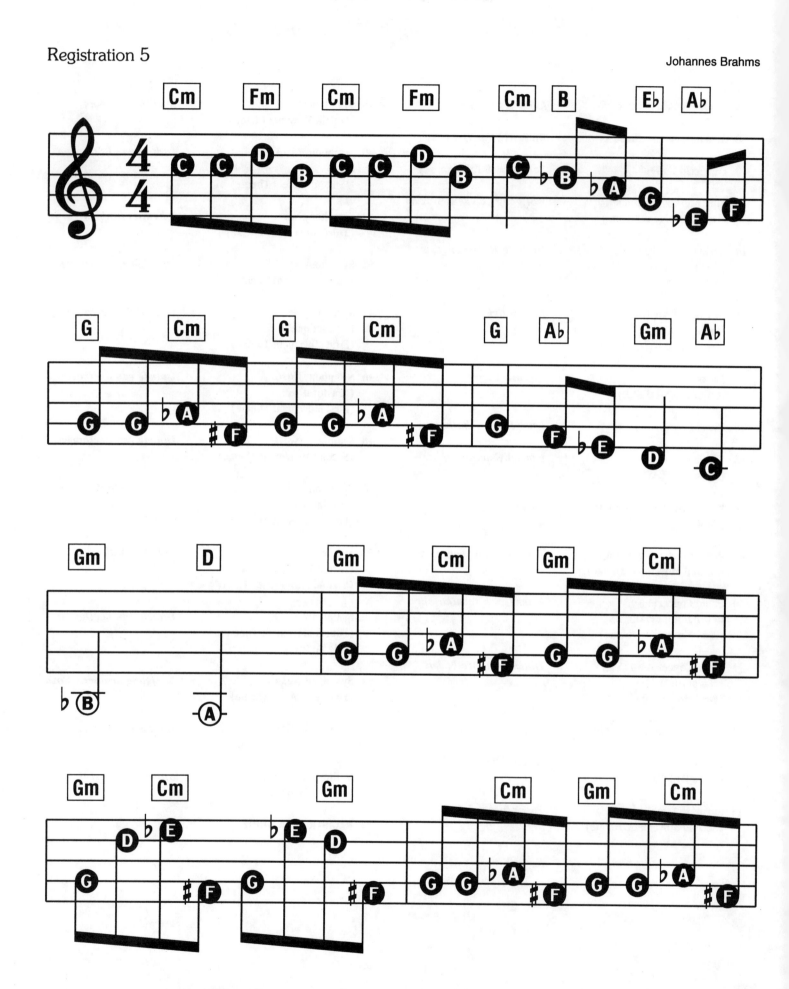

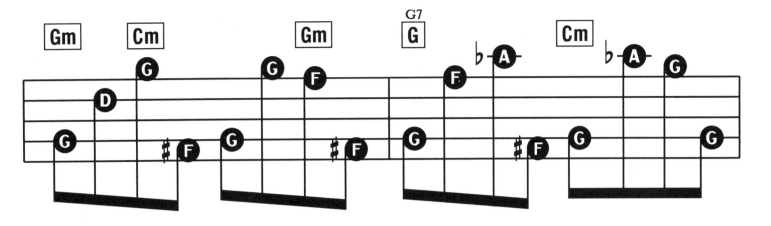
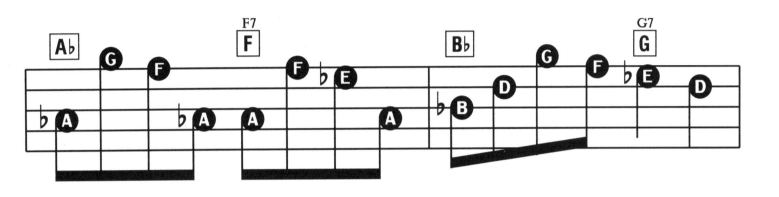
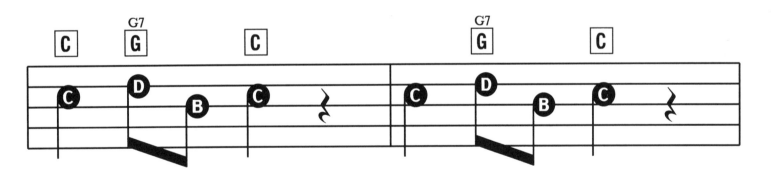
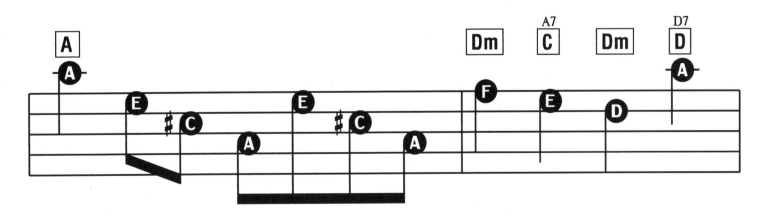

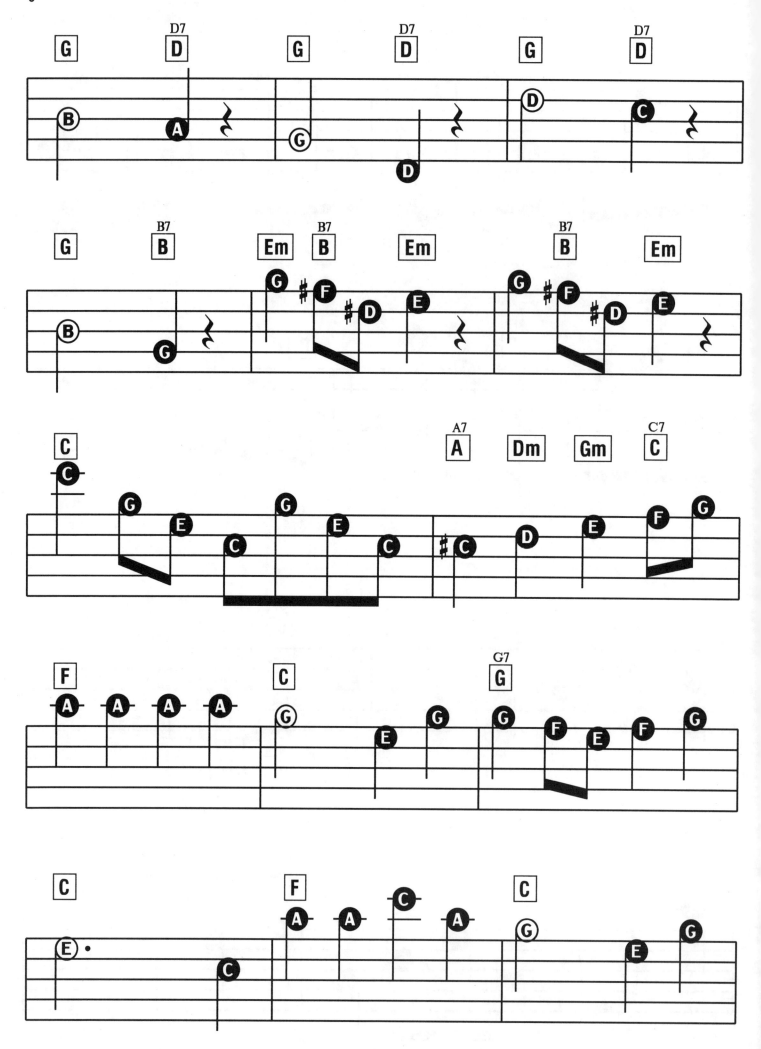

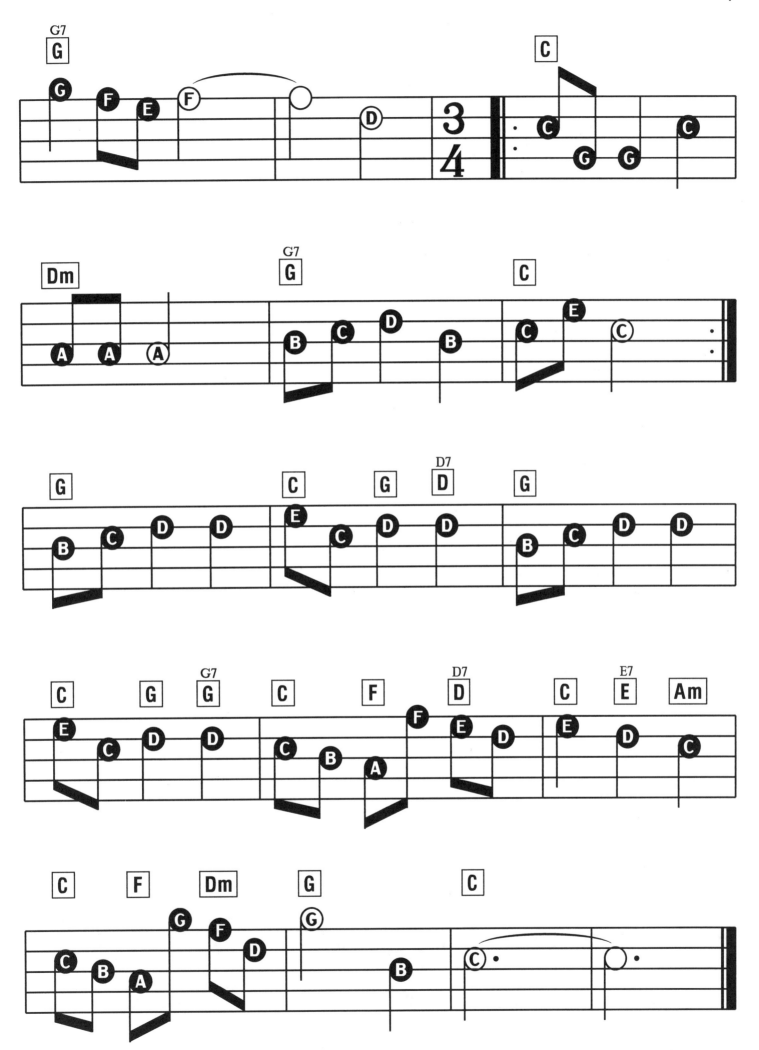

Also Sprach Zarathustra

Registration 2
Rhythm: Rock or Disco

Richard Strauss

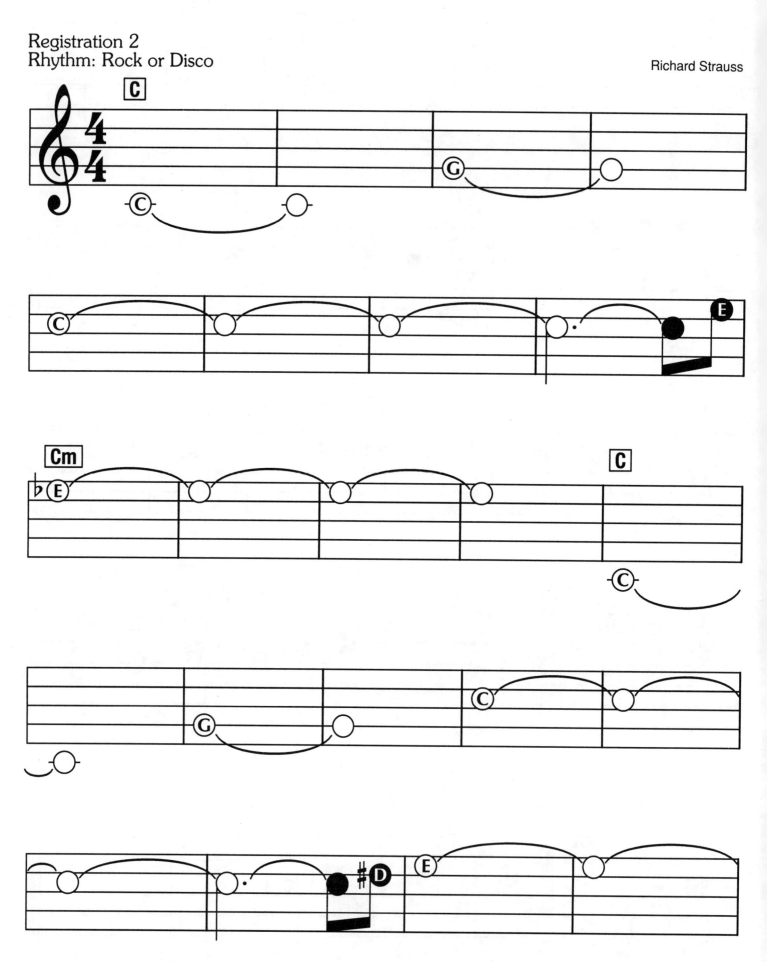

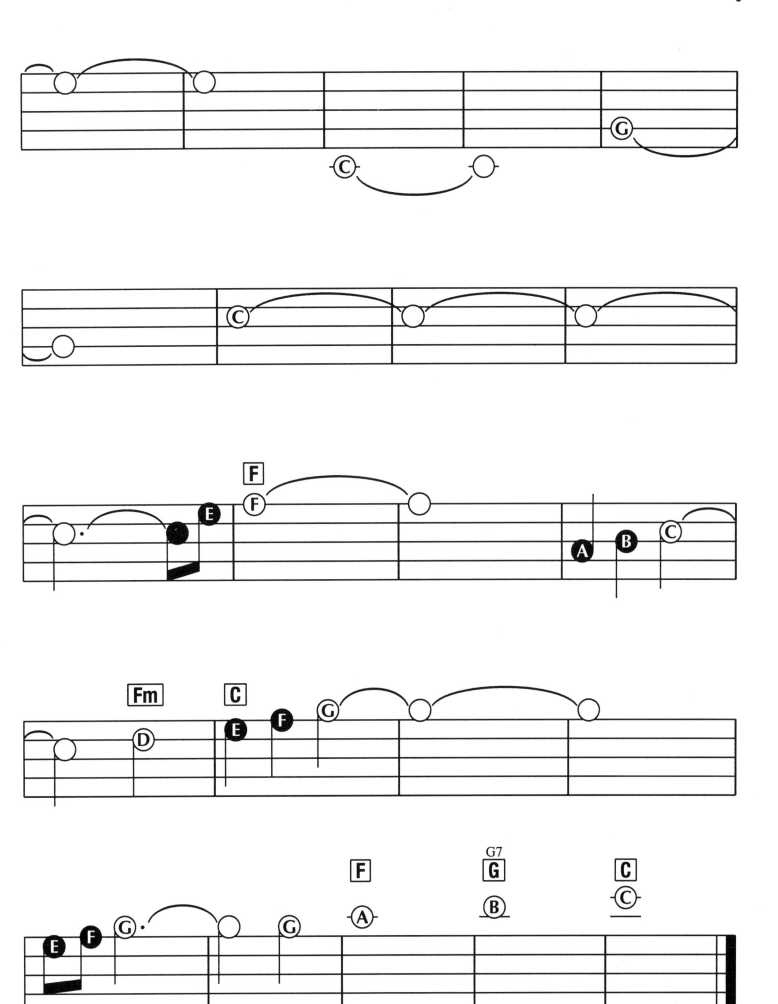

Capriccio Italien

Peter Ilyich Tchaikovsky

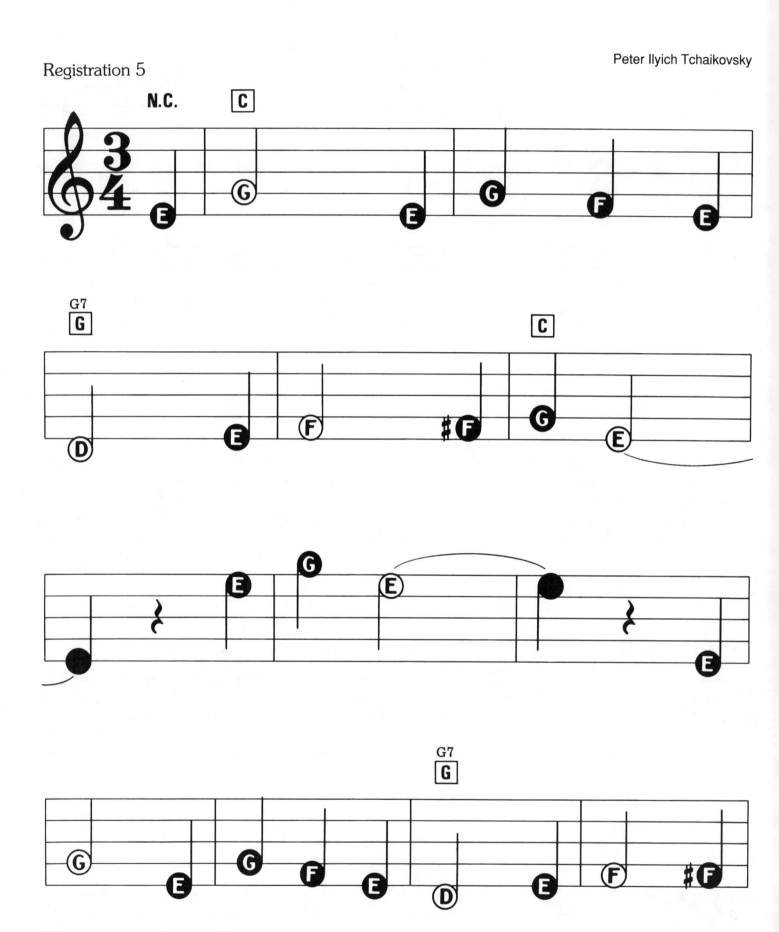

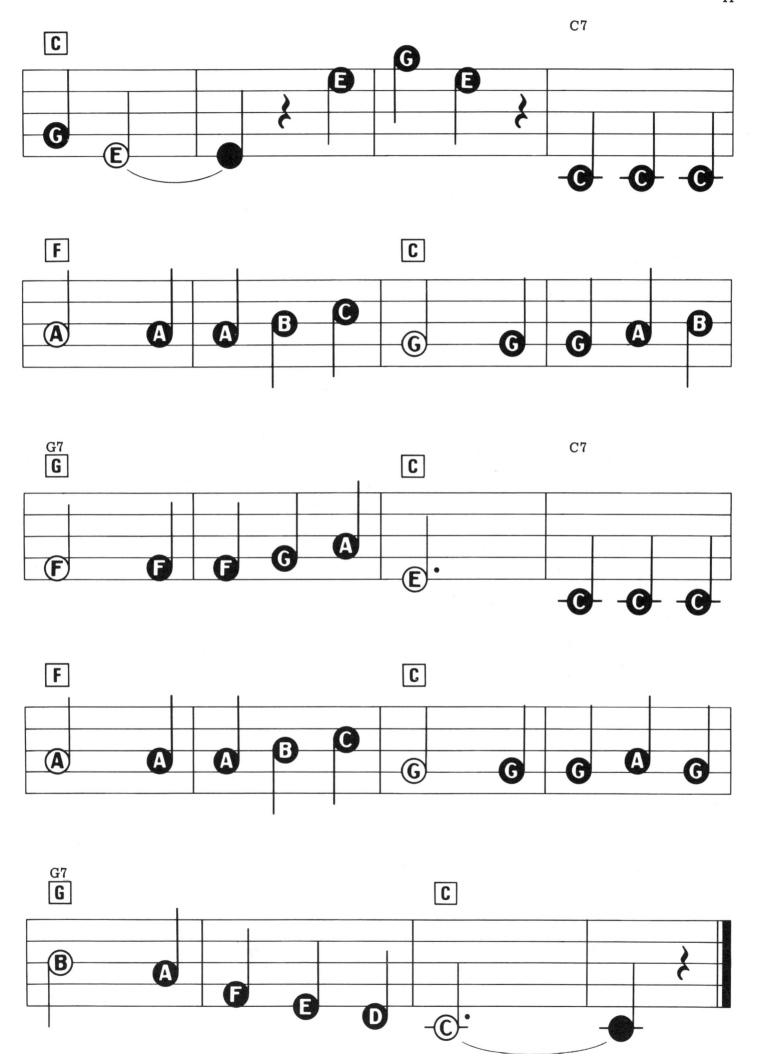

Eine Kleine Nachtmusik
(First Movement Theme)

Registration 3

Wolfgang Amadeus Mozart

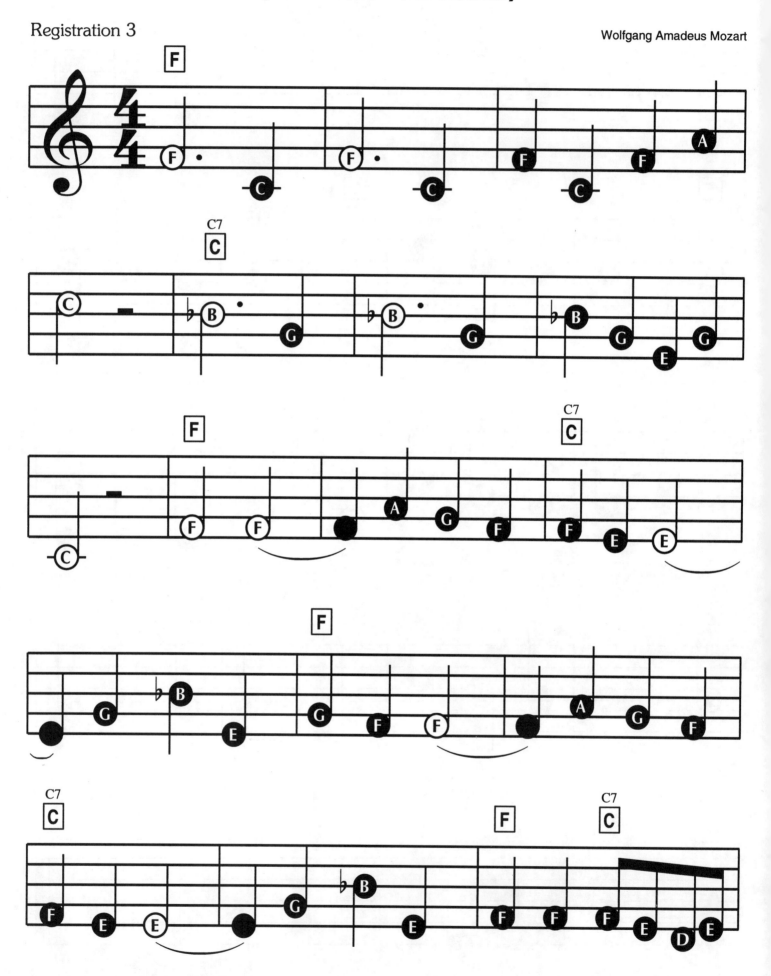

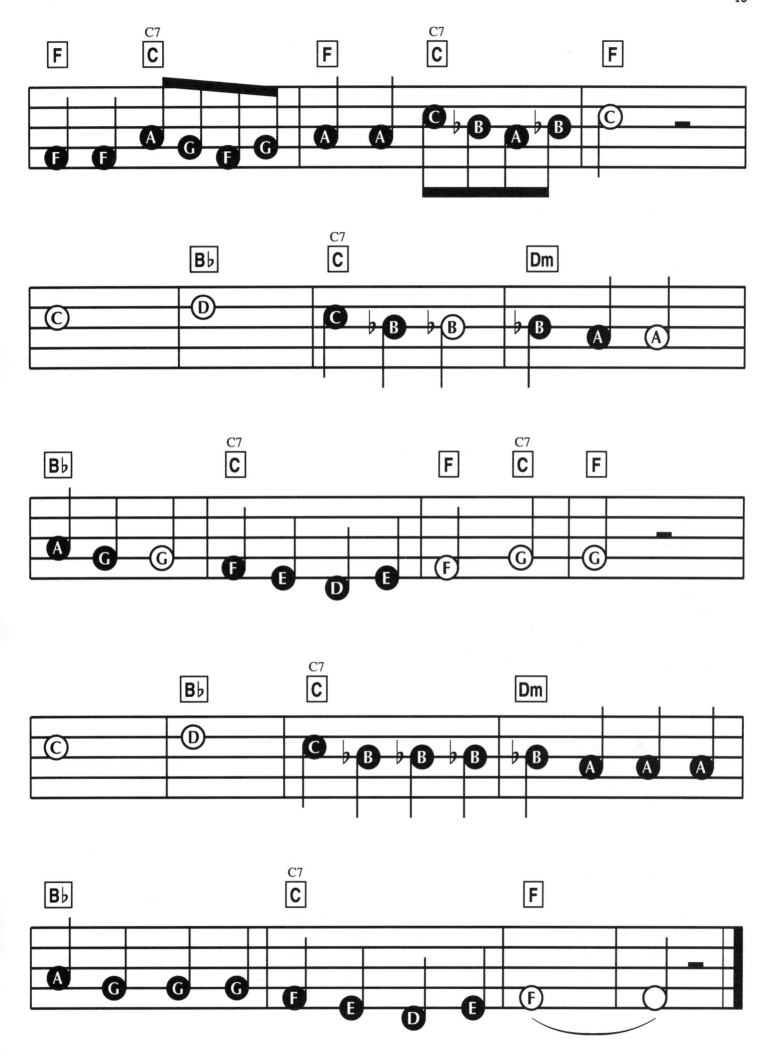

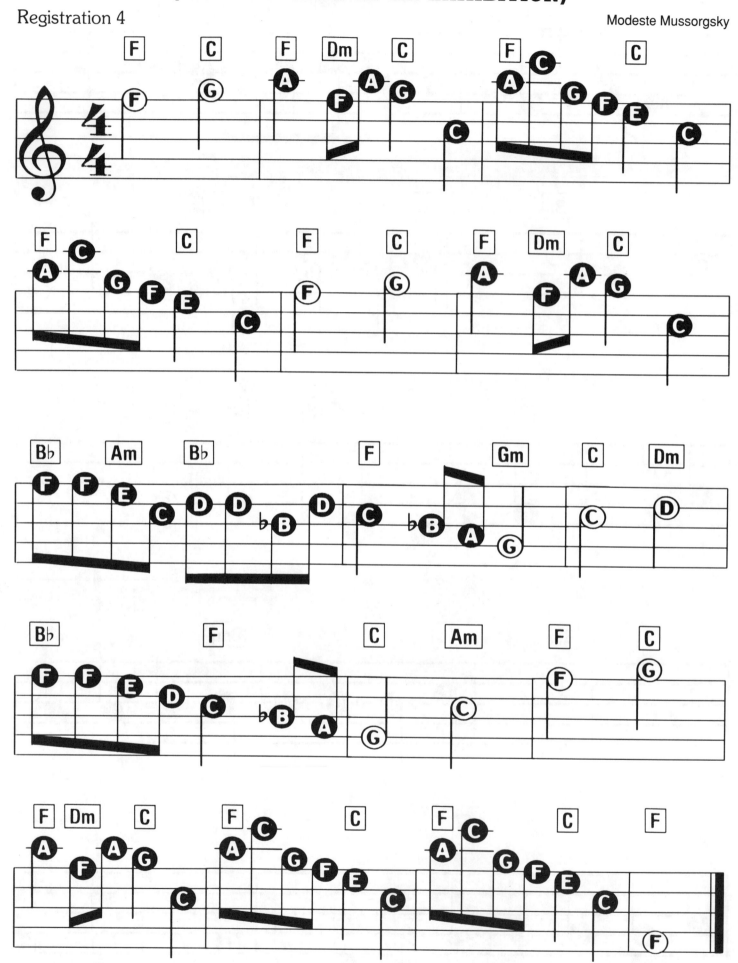

In The Hall Of The Mountain King
(From PEER GYNT SUITE)

Registration 4
Rhythm: Disco

Edvard Grieg

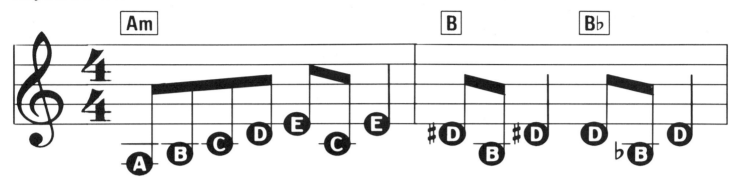
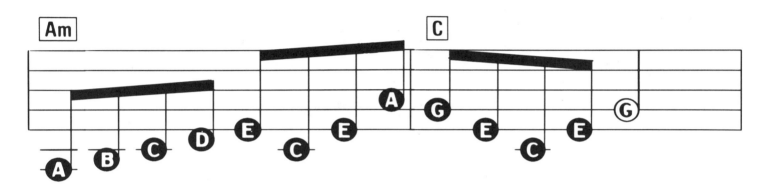
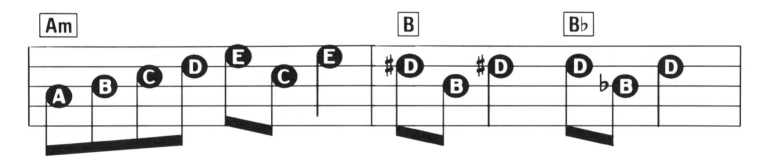
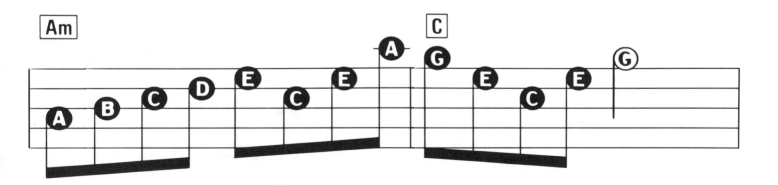

Copyright © 1992 by HAL LEONARD PUBLISHING CORPORATION
International Copyright Secured   All Rights Reserved

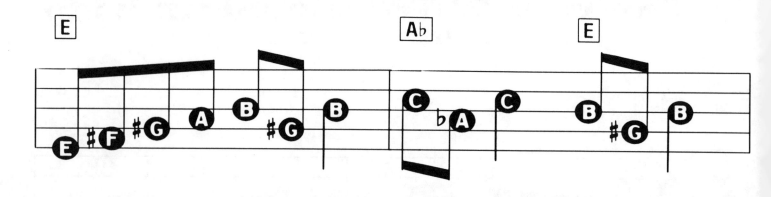
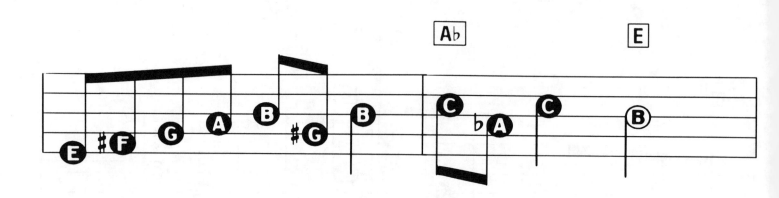
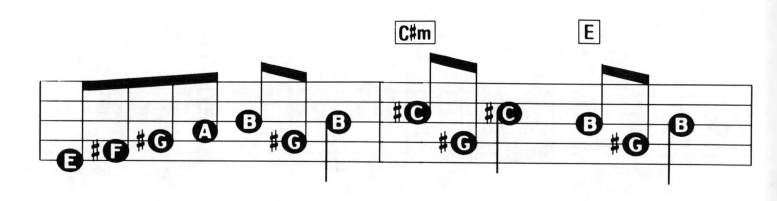
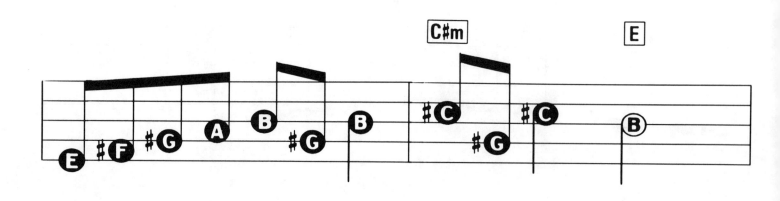

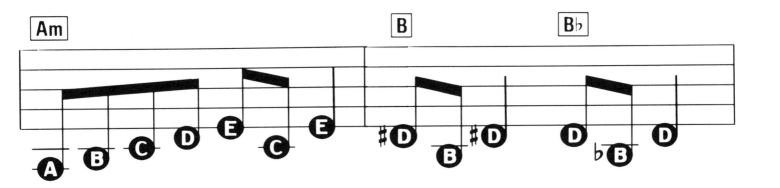
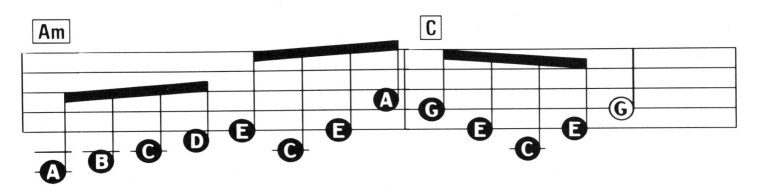
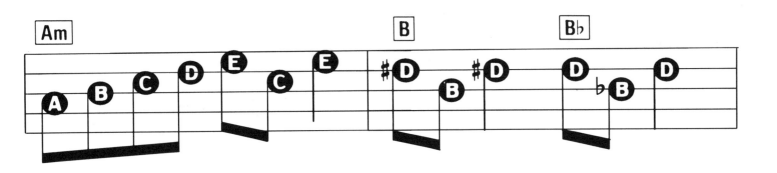
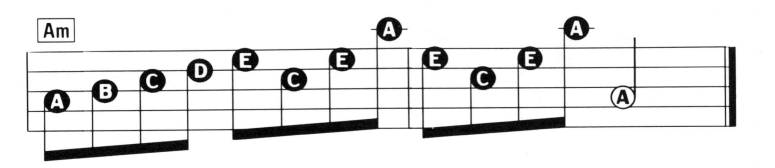

March
(From TANNHAUSER)

Registration 5
Rhythm: March

Richard Wagner

Copyright © 1992 by HAL LEONARD PUBLISHING CORPORATION
International Copyright Secured   All Rights Reserved

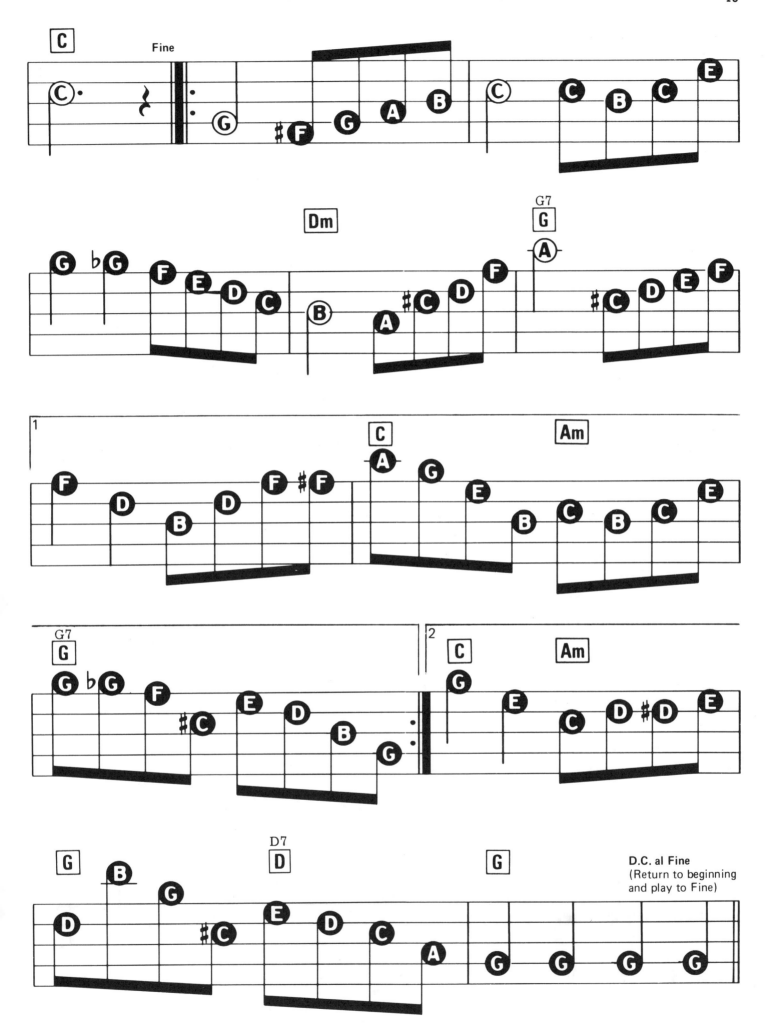

Marche Slav

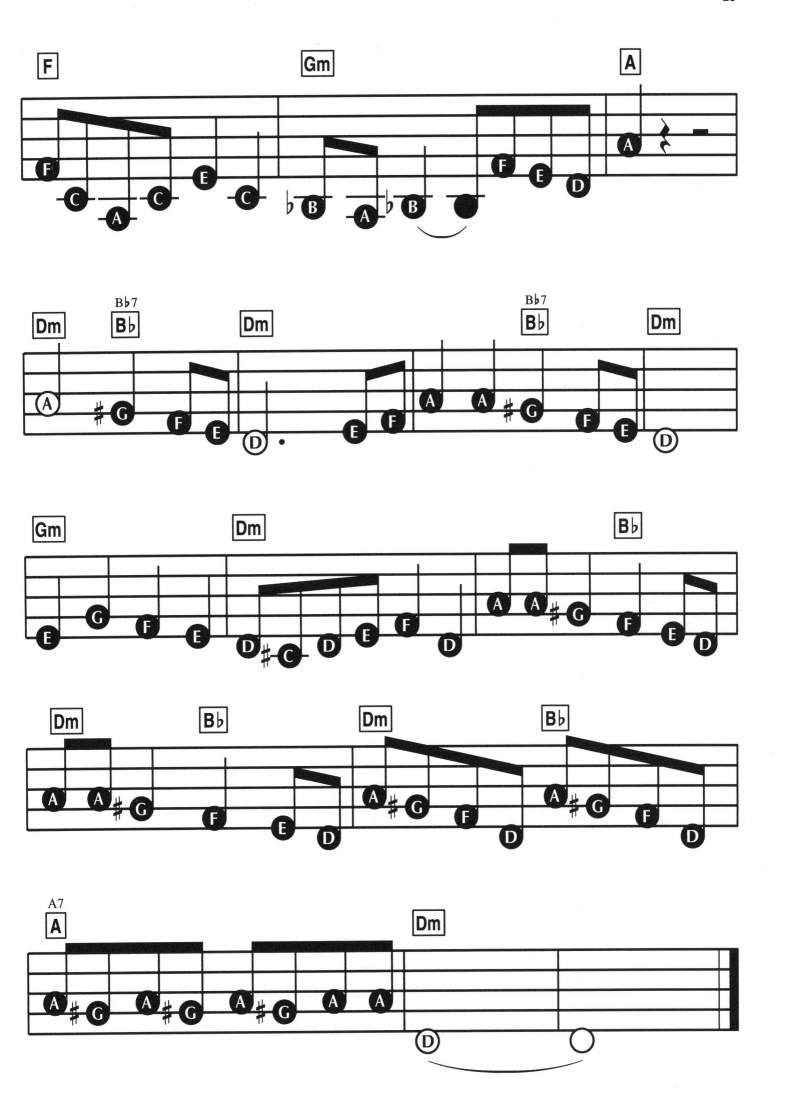

The Moldau
(From MA VLAST)

Registration 10
Rhythm: 6/8 Ballad

Bedrich Smetana

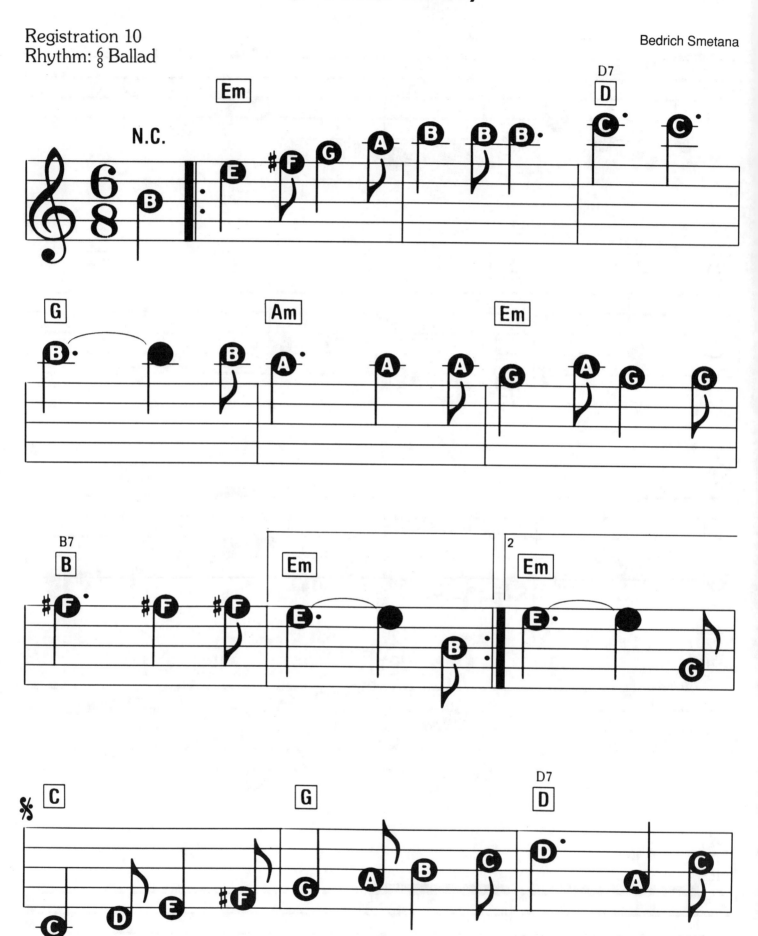

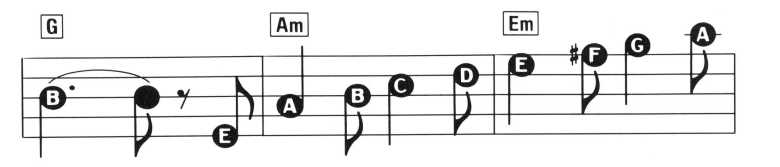
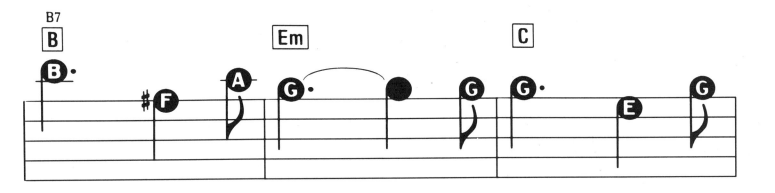
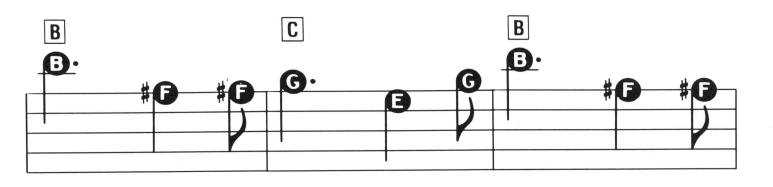
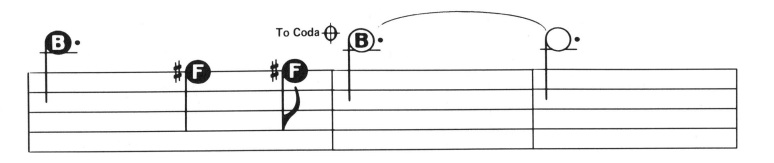

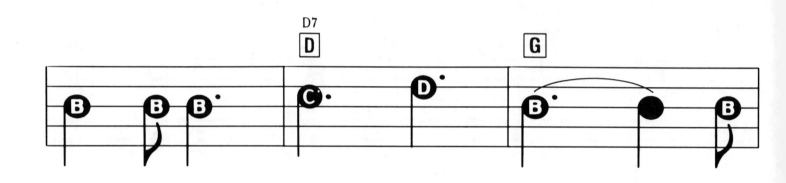
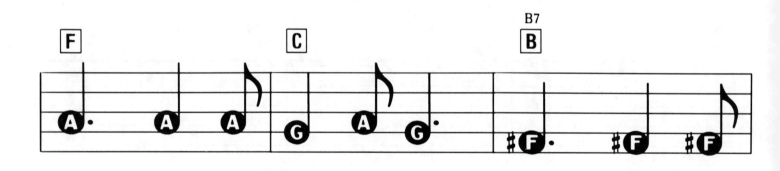
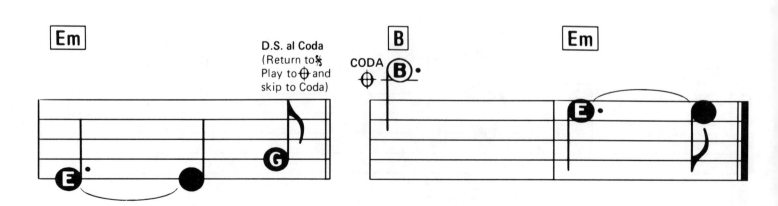

Piano Concerto In C Major
(Second Movement Theme)

Registration 8

Wolfgang Amadeus Mozart

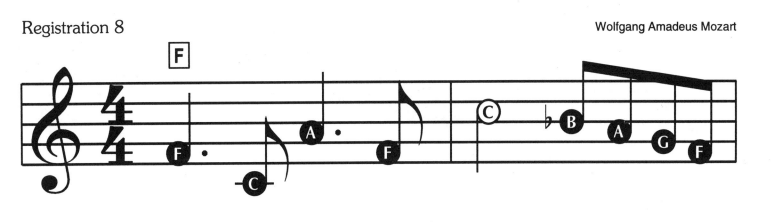

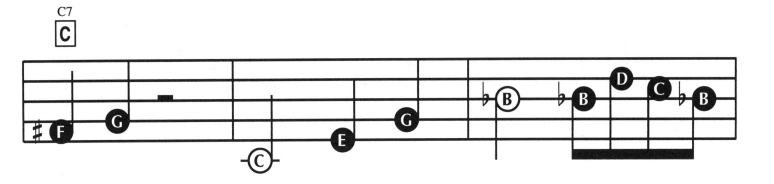

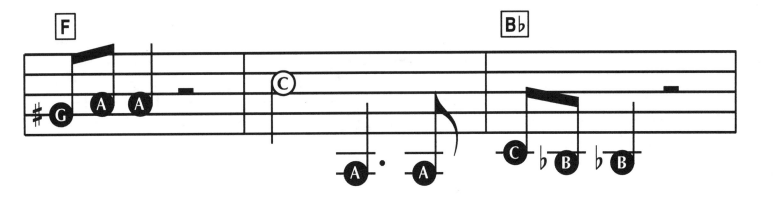

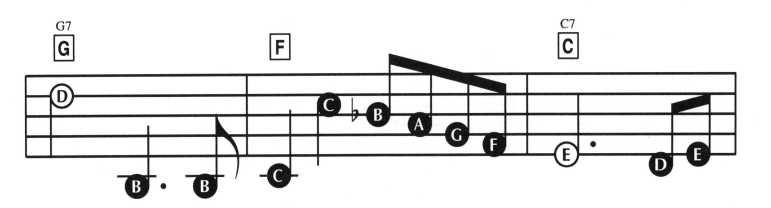

Copyright © 1992 by HAL LEONARD PUBLISHING CORPORATION
International Copyright Secured   All Rights Reserved

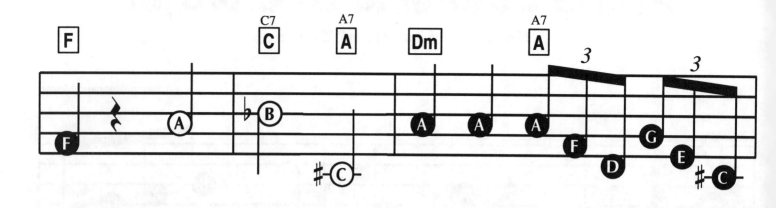
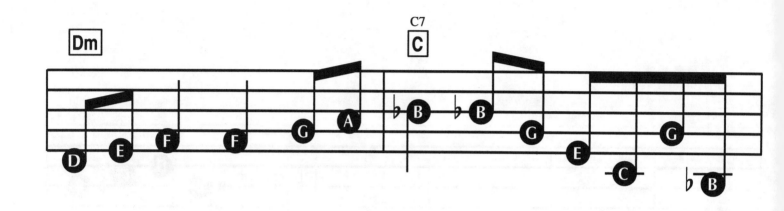
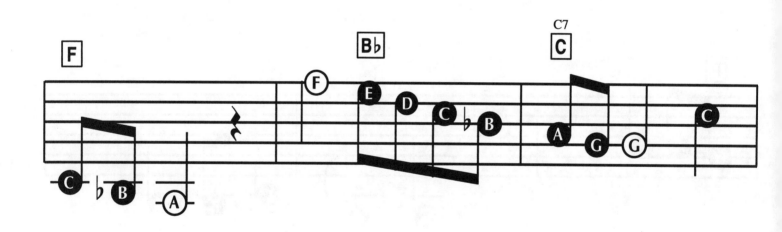
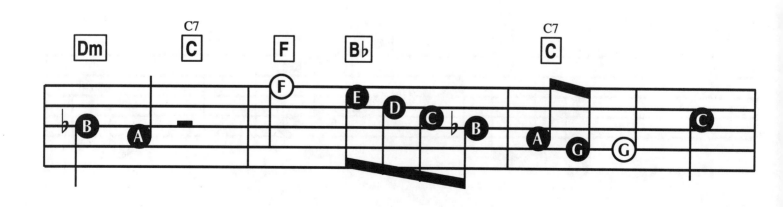

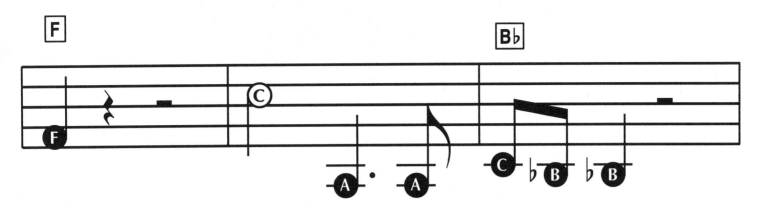
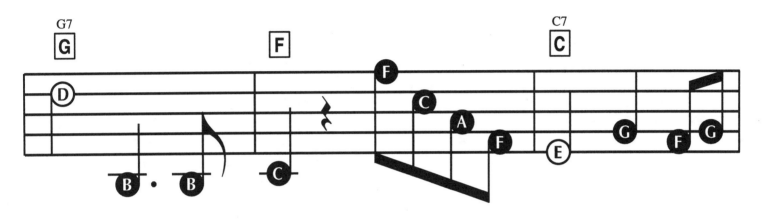
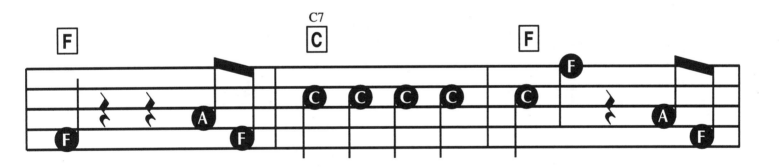
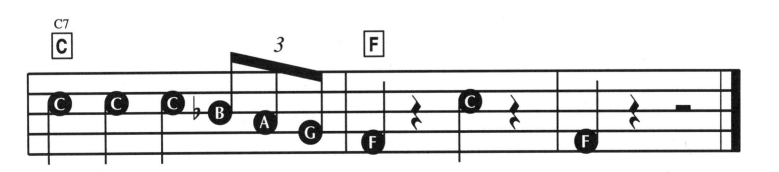

Piano Concerto in A minor
(First Movement Theme)

Registration 8
Rhythm: Swing

Edvard Grieg

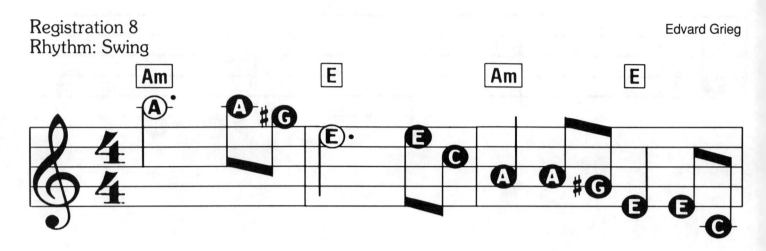
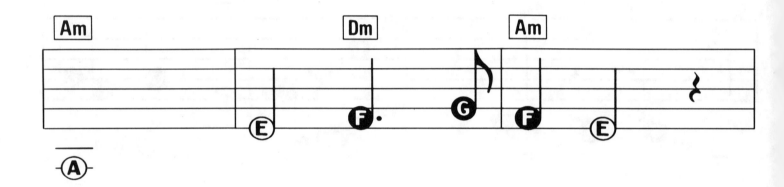
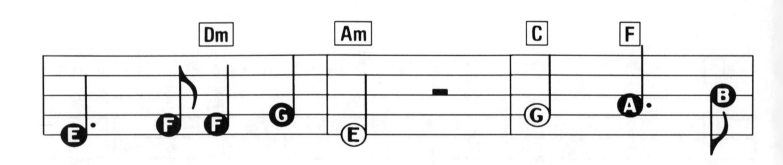
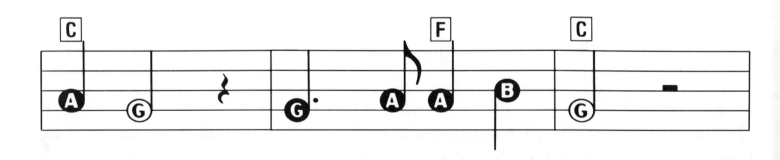

Copyright © 1992 by HAL LEONARD PUBLISHING CORPORATION
International Copyright Secured   All Rights Reserved

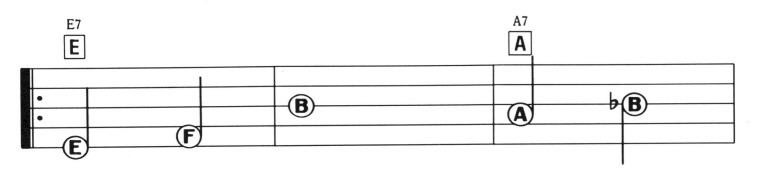
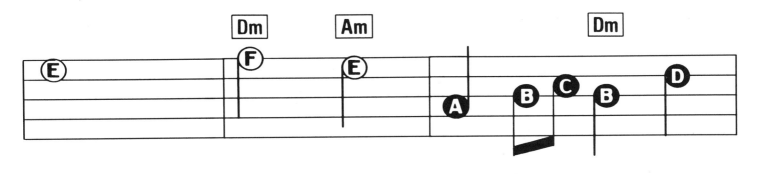
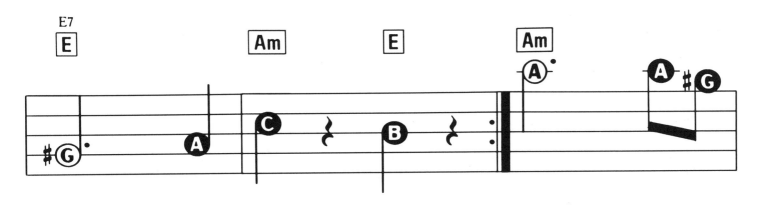
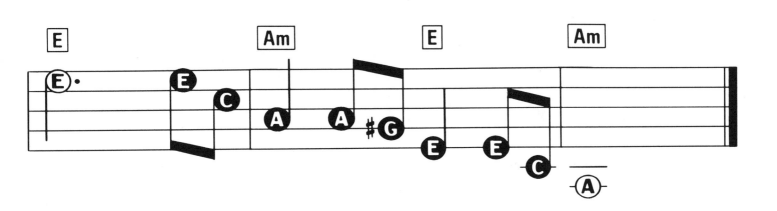

Piano Concerto No. 1 in B-flat minor, Op. 23
(First Movement Theme)

Peter Ilyich Tchaikovsky

Registration 5

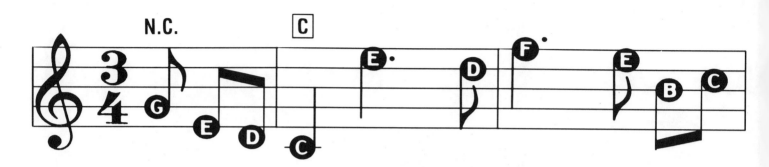

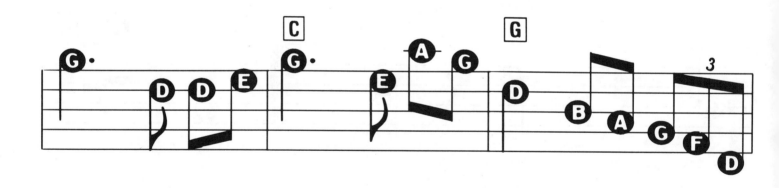

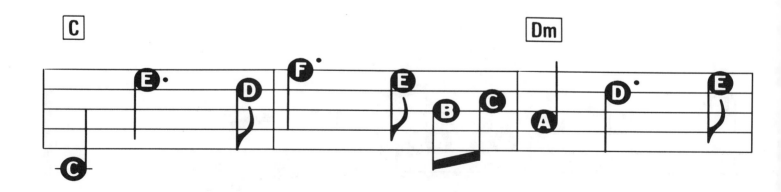

Copyright © 1992 by HAL LEONARD PUBLISHING CORPORATION
International Copyright Secured   All Rights Reserved

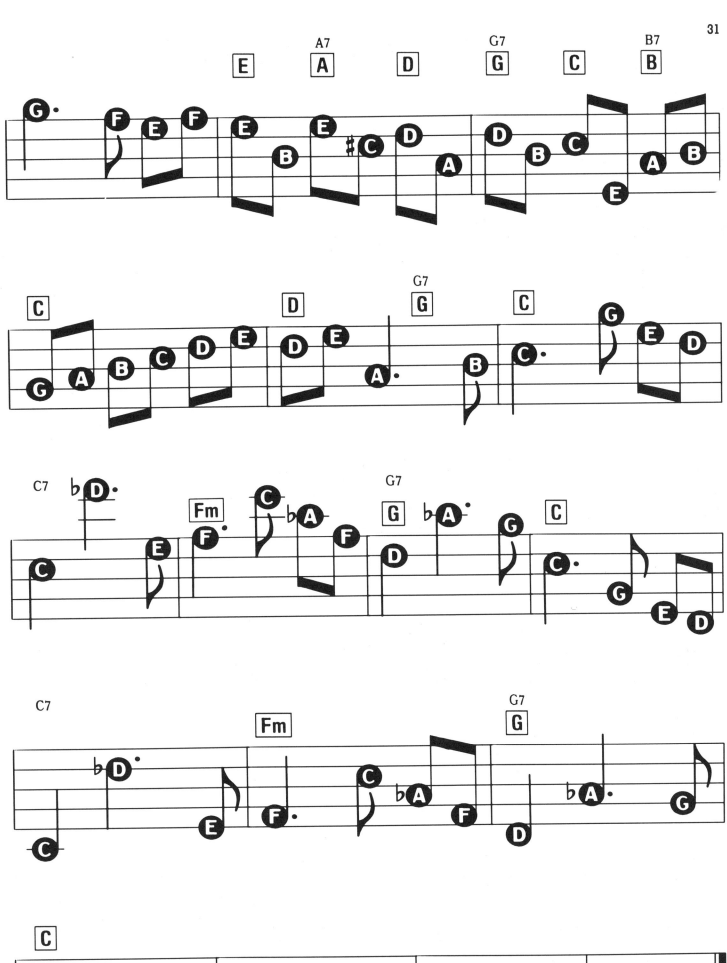
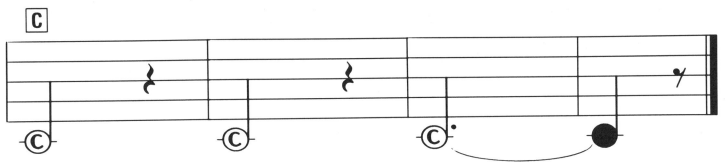

Poet And Peasant Overture

Registration 9

Franz von Suppe

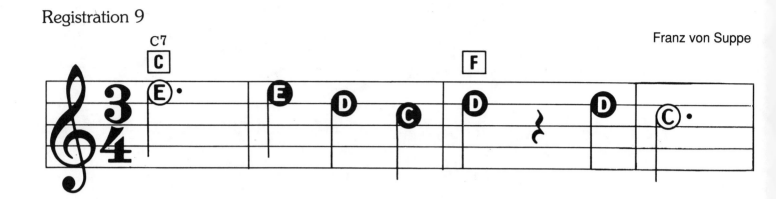
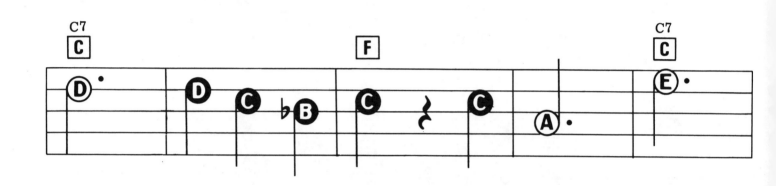
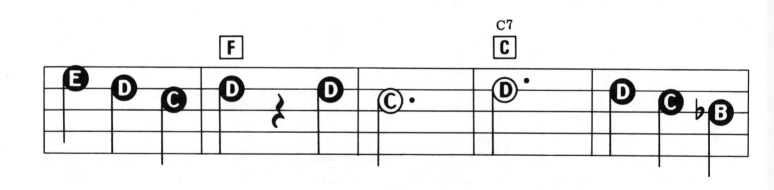
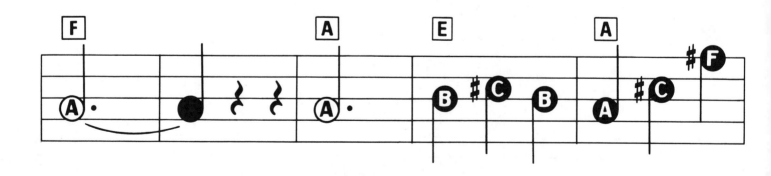

Copyright © 1992 by HAL LEONARD PUBLISHING CORPORATION
International Copyright Secured   All Rights Reserved

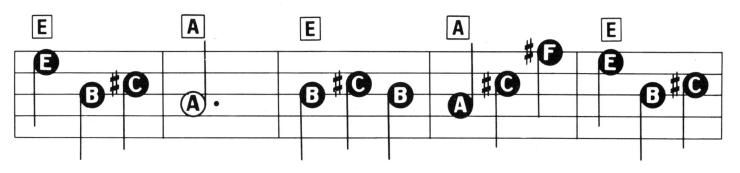
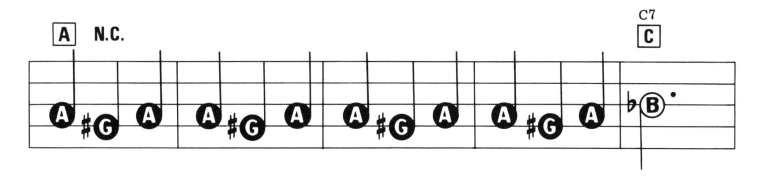
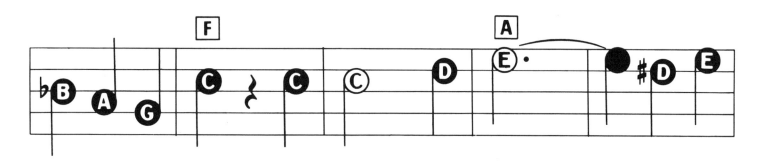
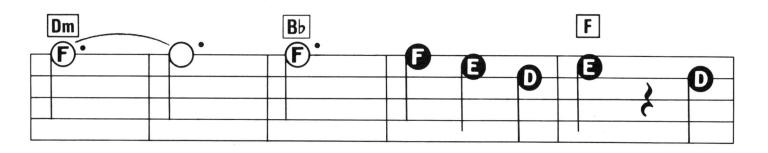
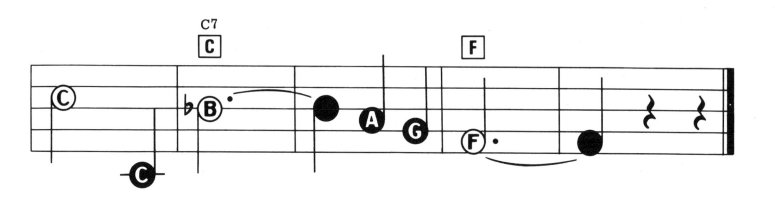

Piano Concerto No. 5
("Emperor")
(First Movement)

Registration 8
Rhythm: March (Optional)

Ludwig van Beethoven

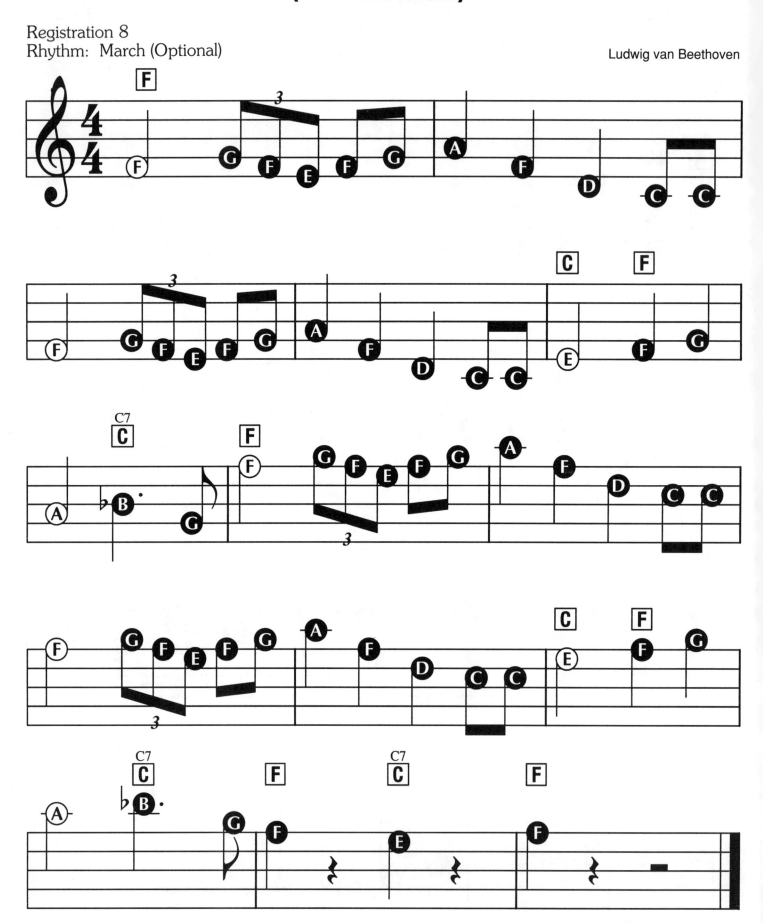

Copyright © 1992 by HAL LEONARD PUBLISHING CORPORATION
International Copyright Secured   All Rights Reserved

Surprise Symphony
(Second Movement Theme)

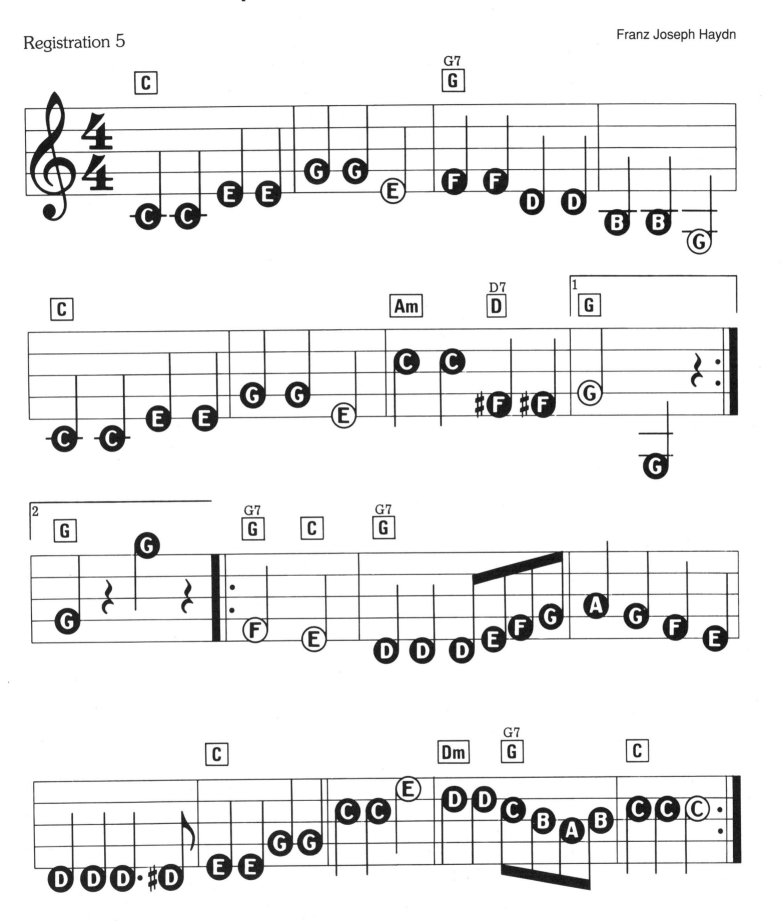

Ride Of The Valkyries
(From DIE WALKURE)

Registration 5
Rhythm: Waltz

Richard Wagner

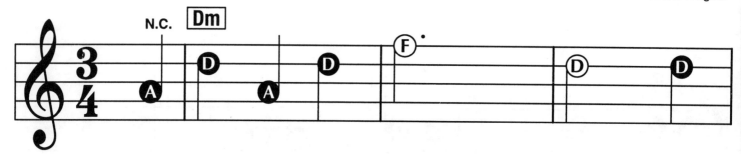

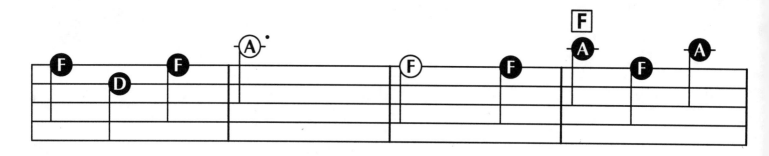

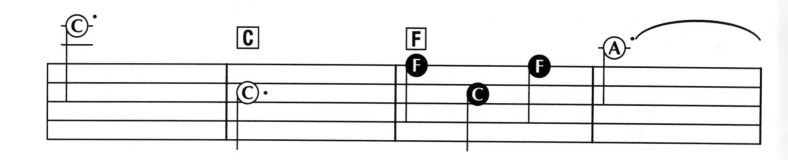

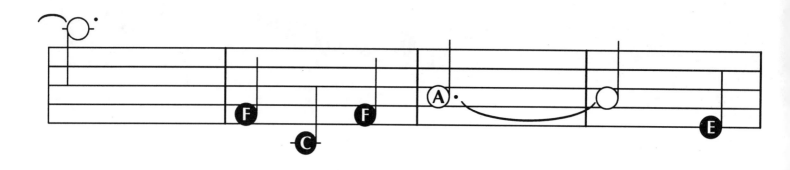

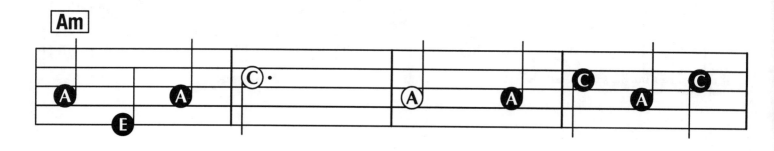

Copyright © 1992 by HAL LEONARD PUBLISHING CORPORATION
International Copyright Secured   All Rights Reserved

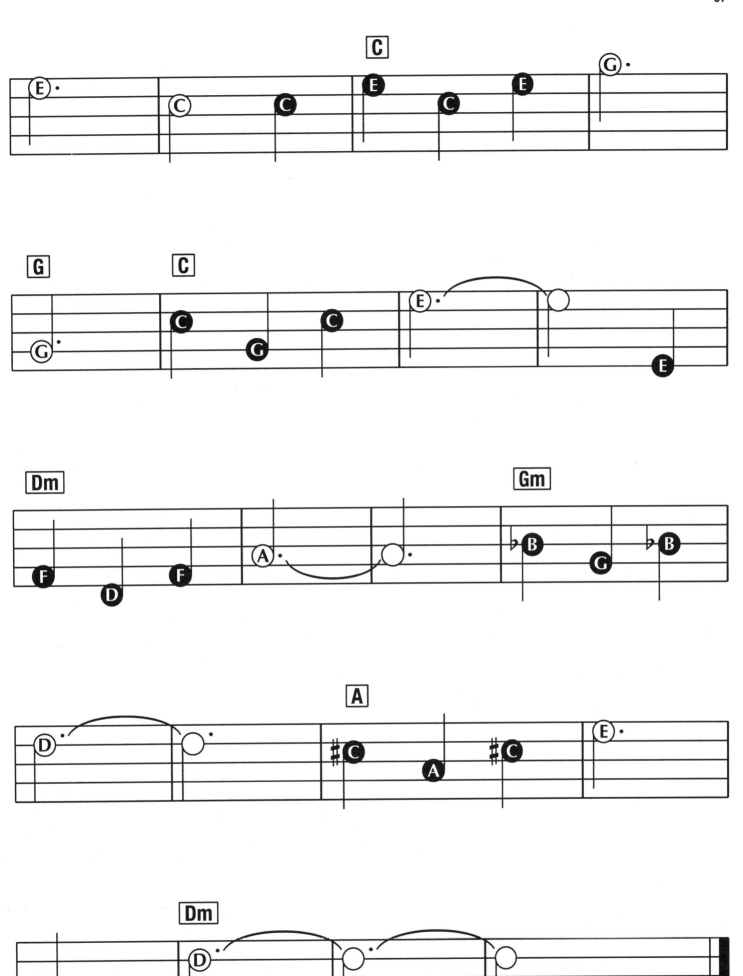

Symphony No. 1
(Fourth Movement Chorale)

Registration 3

Johannes Brahms

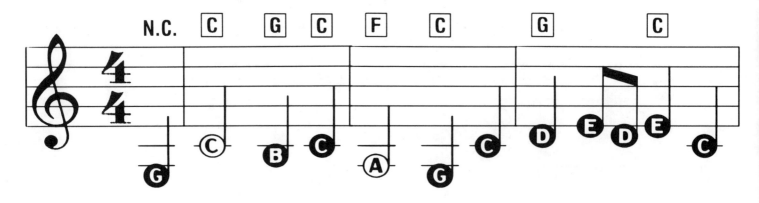
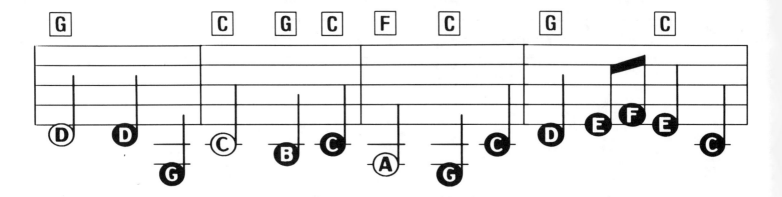
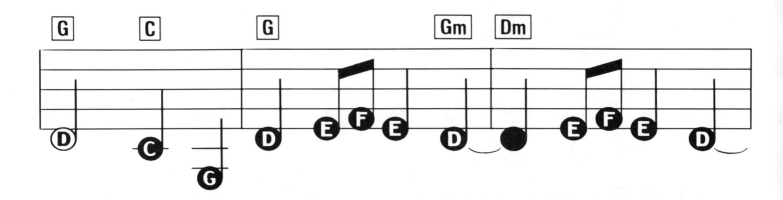
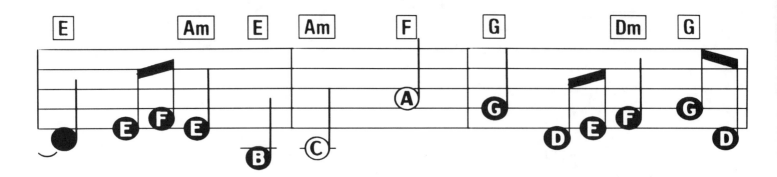

Copyright © 1992 by HAL LEONARD PUBLISHING CORPORATION
International Copyright Secured All Rights Reserved

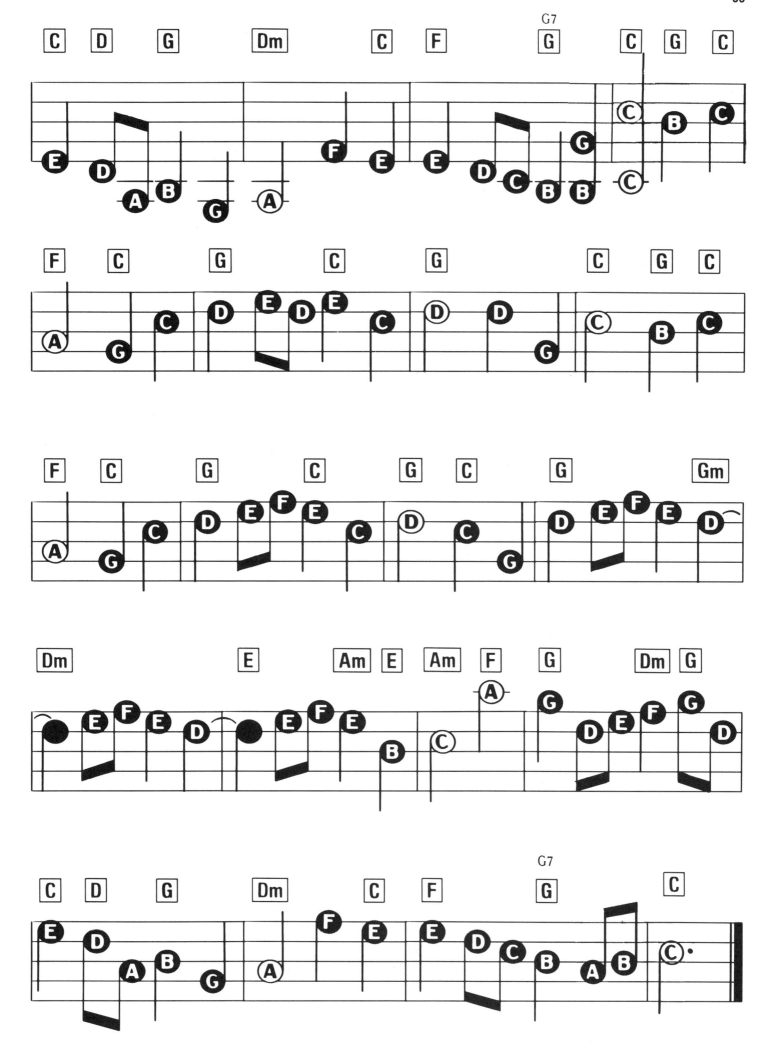

Symphony No. 3
("Eroica")
(First Movement Theme)

Registration 3

Ludwig van Beethoven

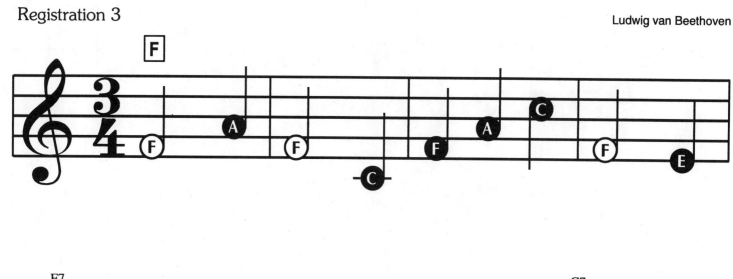

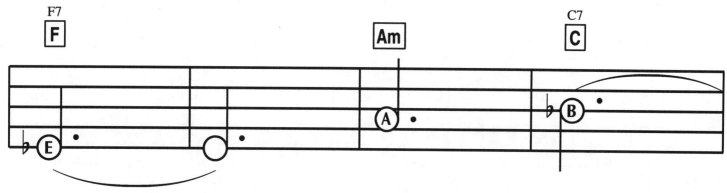

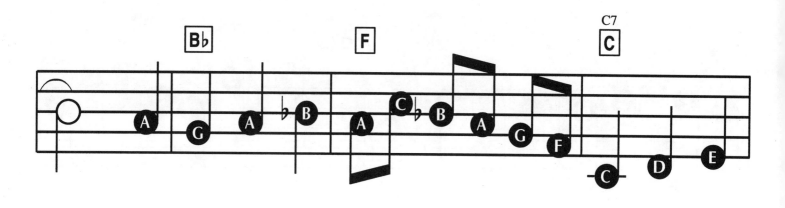

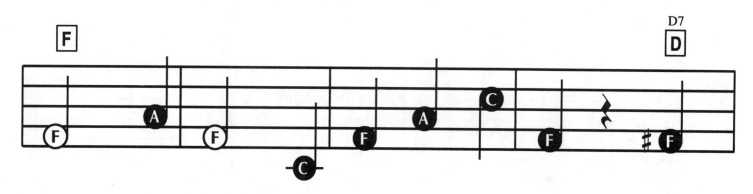

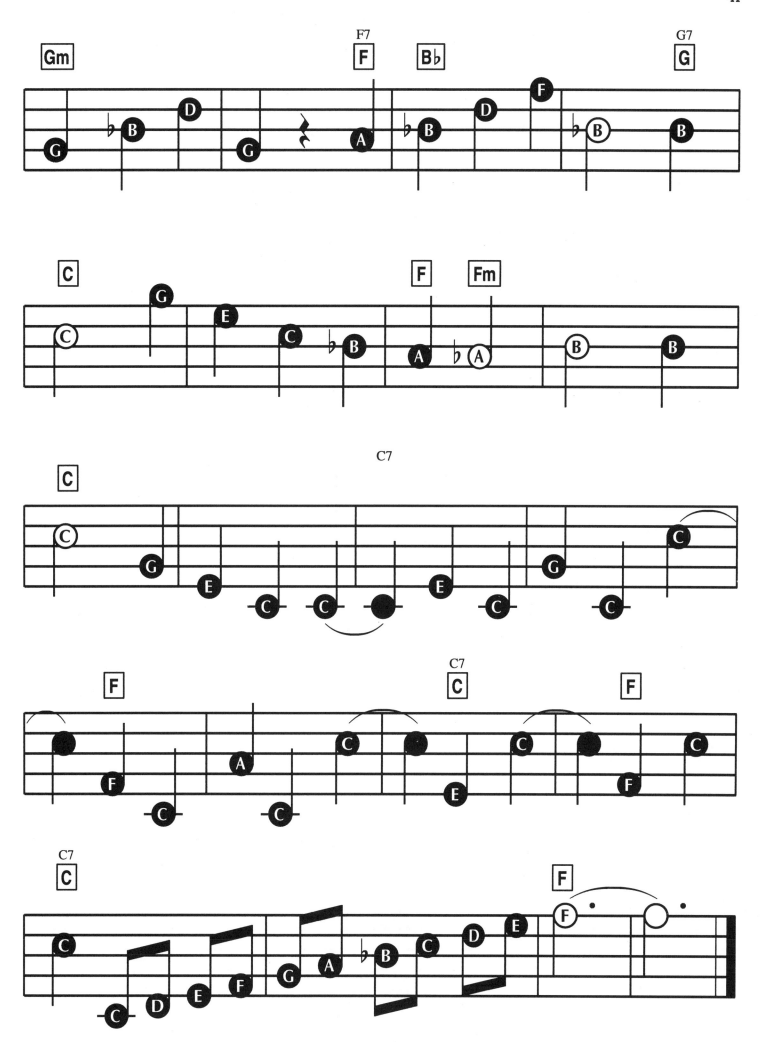

Symphony No. 4
(Third Movement Theme)

Registration 4
Rhythm: March or Polka

Johannes Brahms

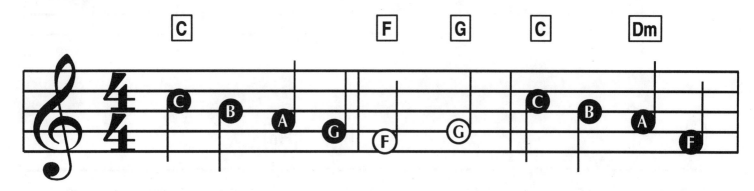
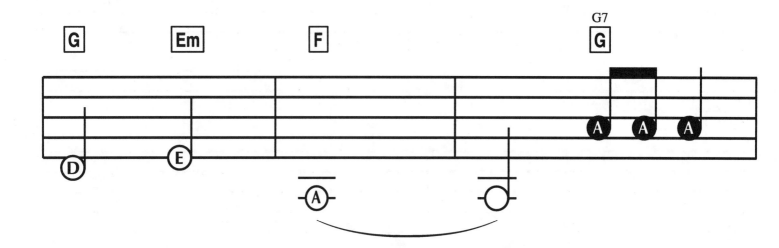
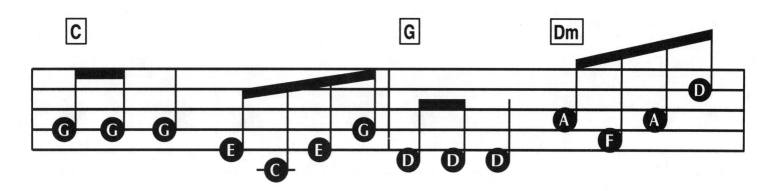
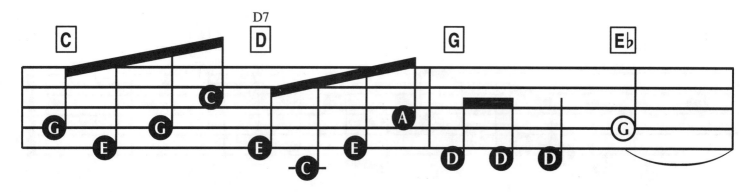

Copyright © 1992 by HAL LEONARD PUBLISHING CORPORATION
International Copyright Secured   All Rights Reserved

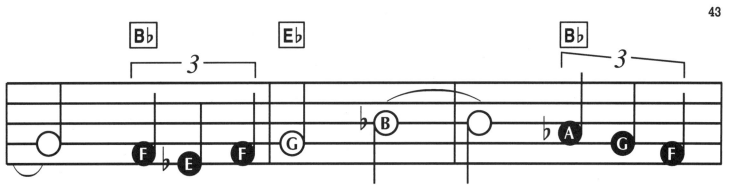
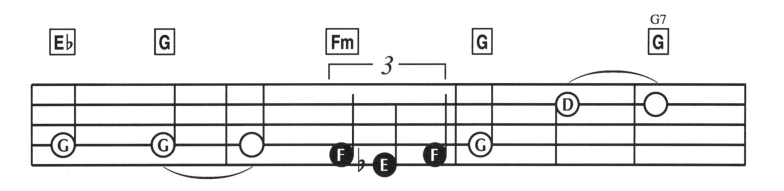
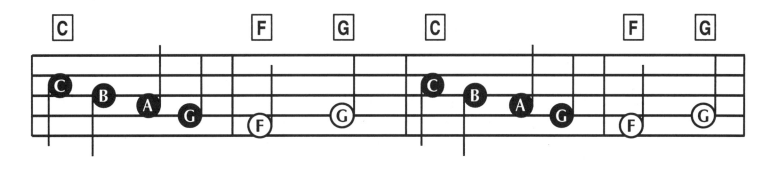
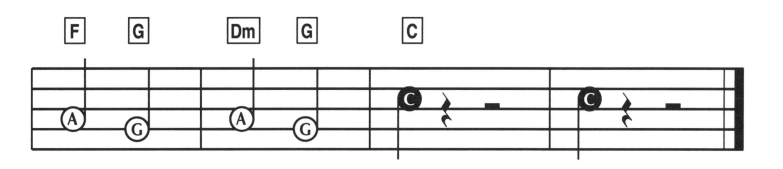

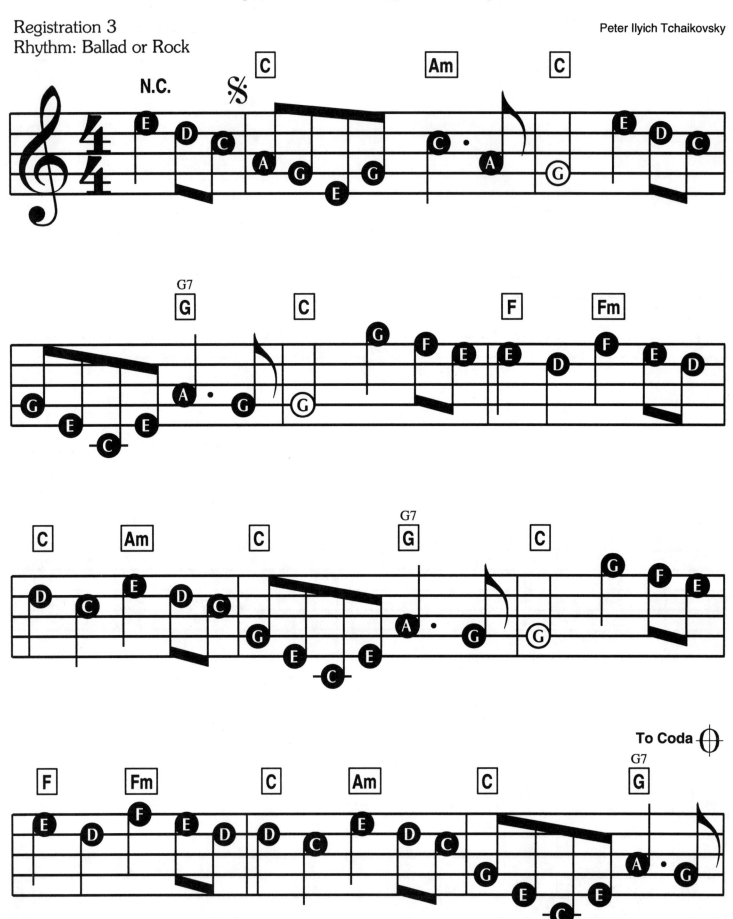

Symphony No. 6

("Pastoral")
(First Movement Theme)

Registration 1

Ludwig van Beethoven

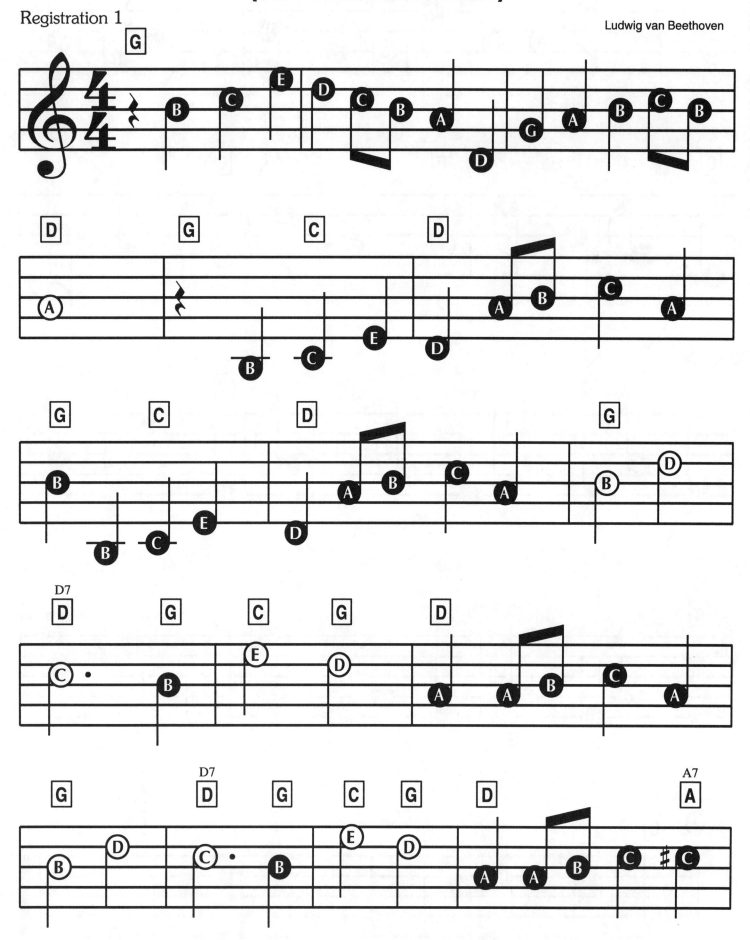

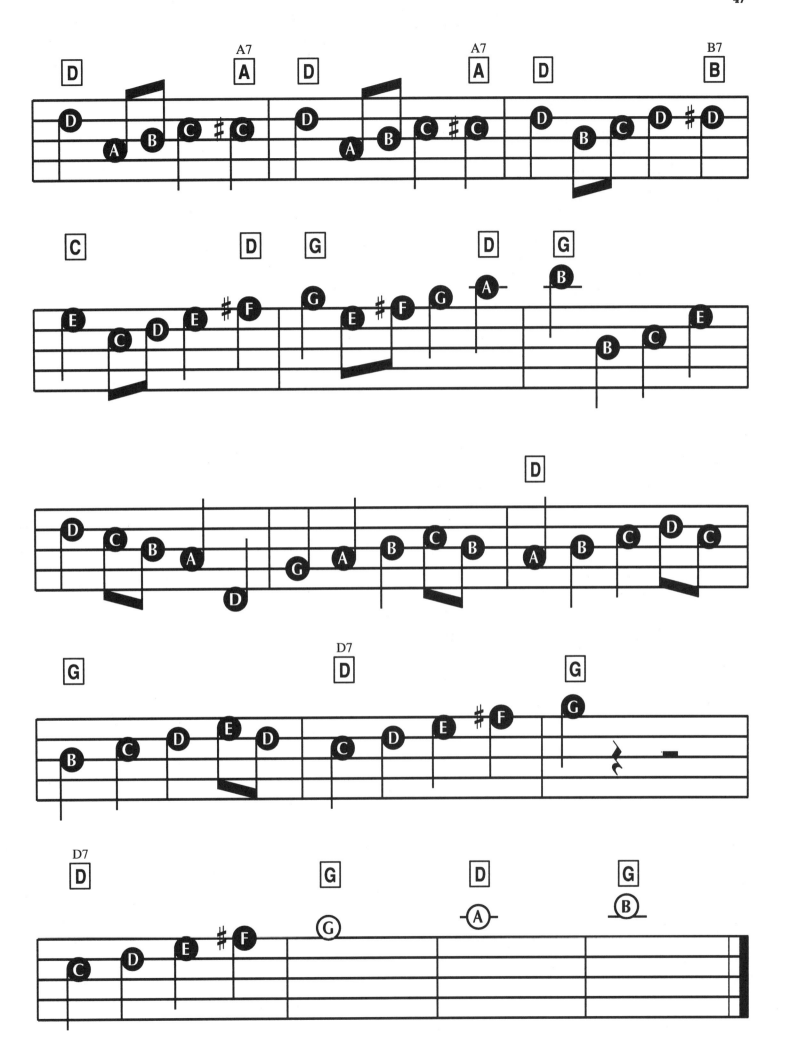

Symphony No. 7
(Second Movement Theme)

Registration 3
Rhythm: Rock

Ludwig van Beethoven

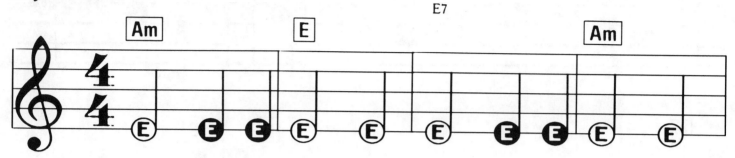

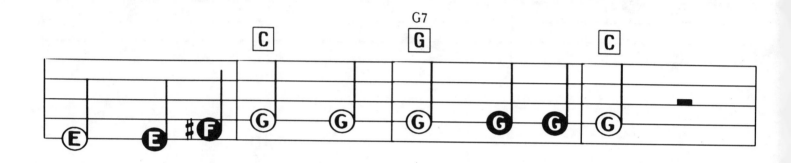

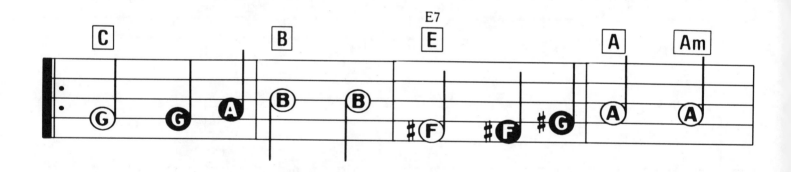

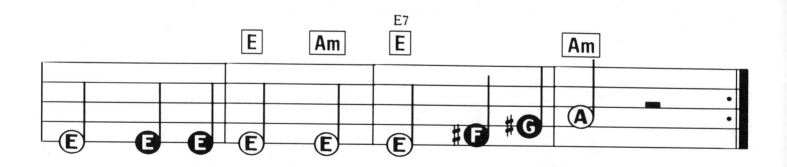

Copyright © 1992 by HAL LEONARD PUBLISHING CORPORATION
International Copyright Secured   All Rights Reserved

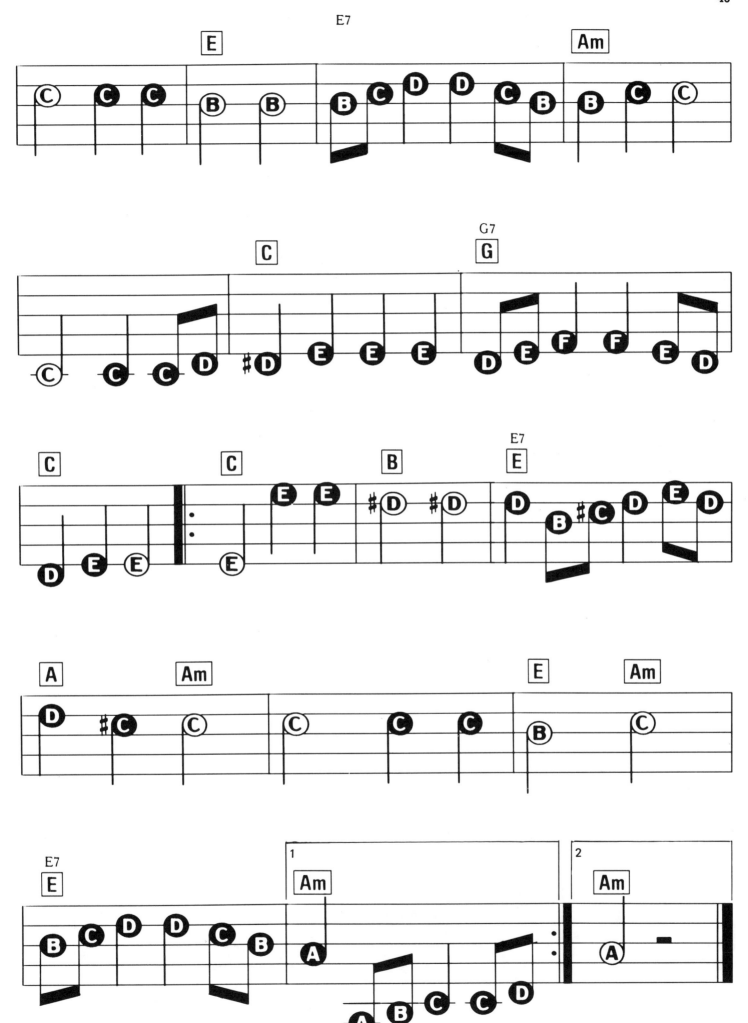

Symphony No. 8
("Unfinished")
(First Movement Theme)

Registration 3
Rhythm: Waltz

Franz Schubert

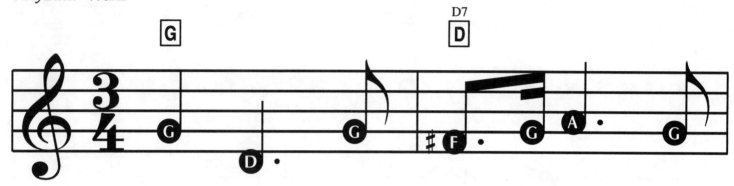
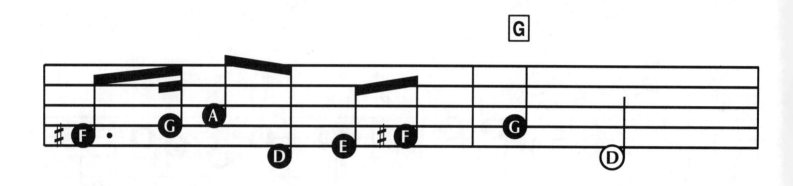
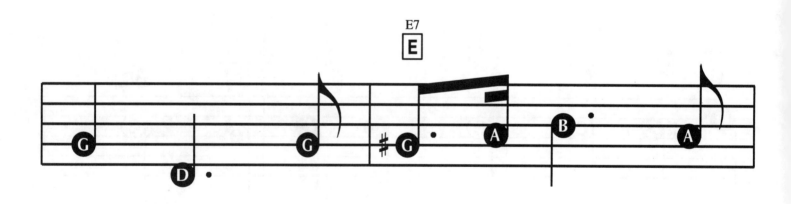

Copyright © 1992 by HAL LEONARD PUBLISHING CORPORATION
International Copyright Secured   All Rights Reserved

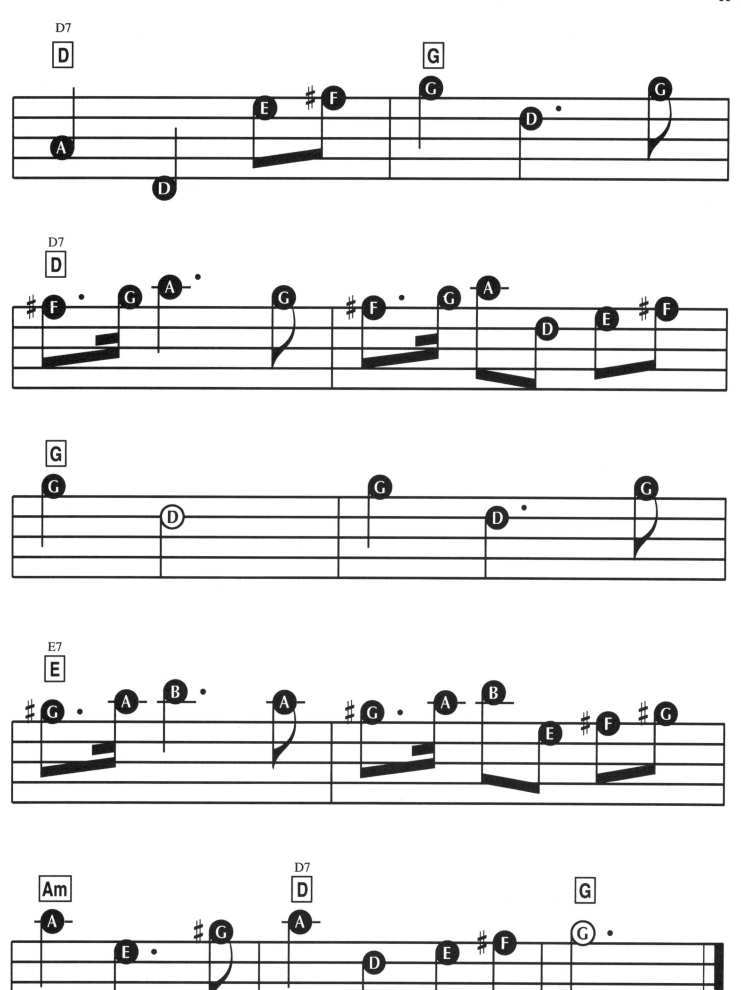

Symphony No. 5
(First Movement Theme)

Registration 3

Ludwig van Beethoven

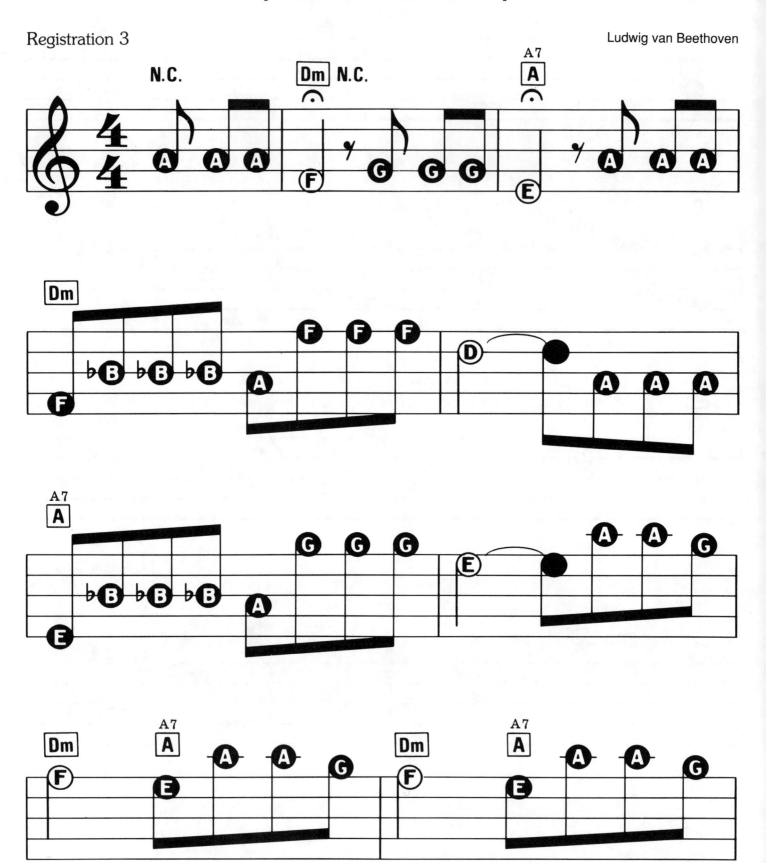

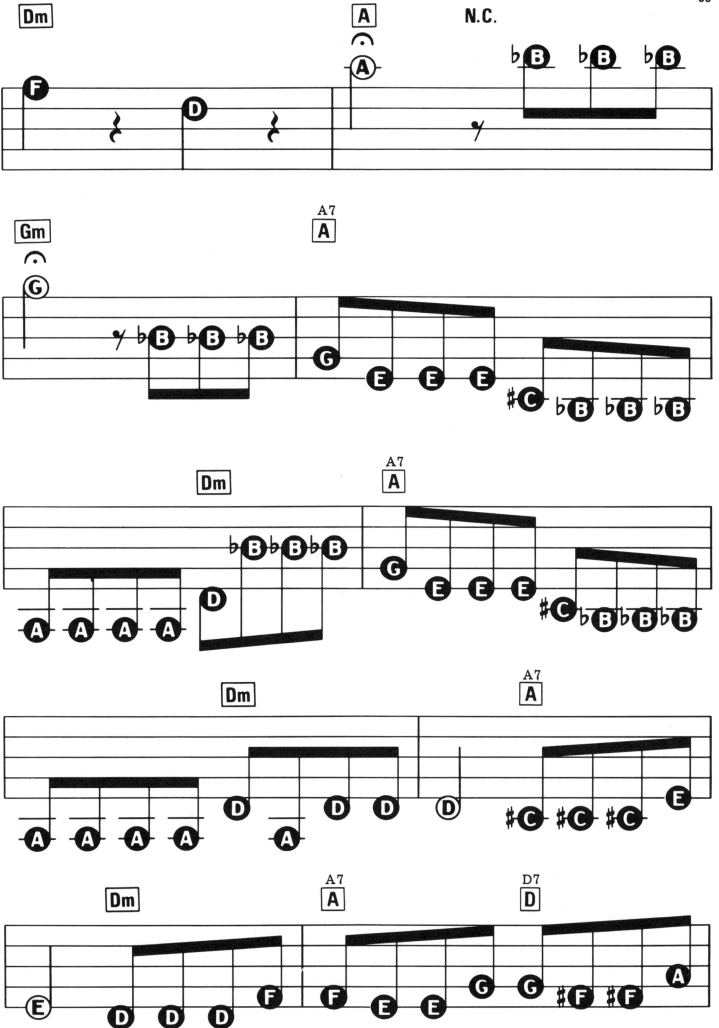

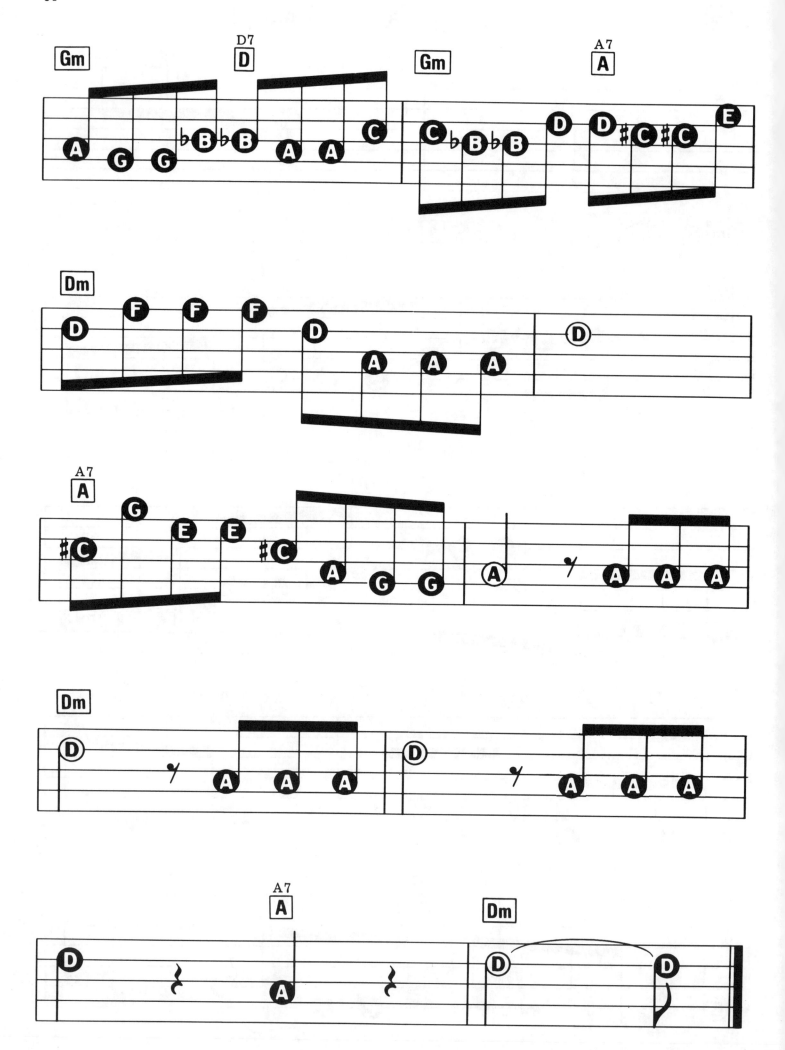

Symphony No. 9
("From The New World")
(Second Movement, "Largo")

Anton Dvorak

Registration 2

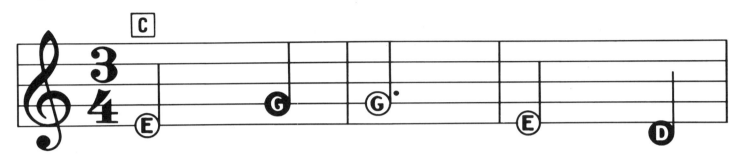

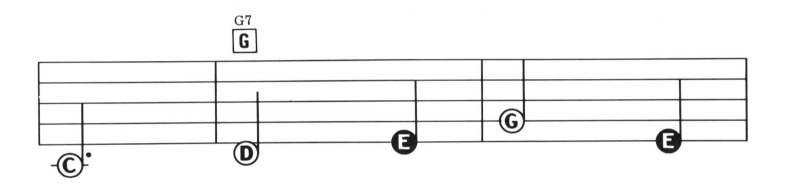

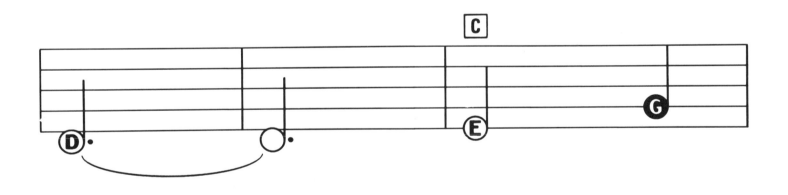

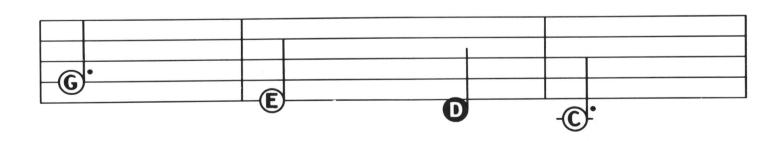

Copyright © 1992 by HAL LEONARD PUBLISHING CORPORATION
International Copyright Secured   All Rights Reserved

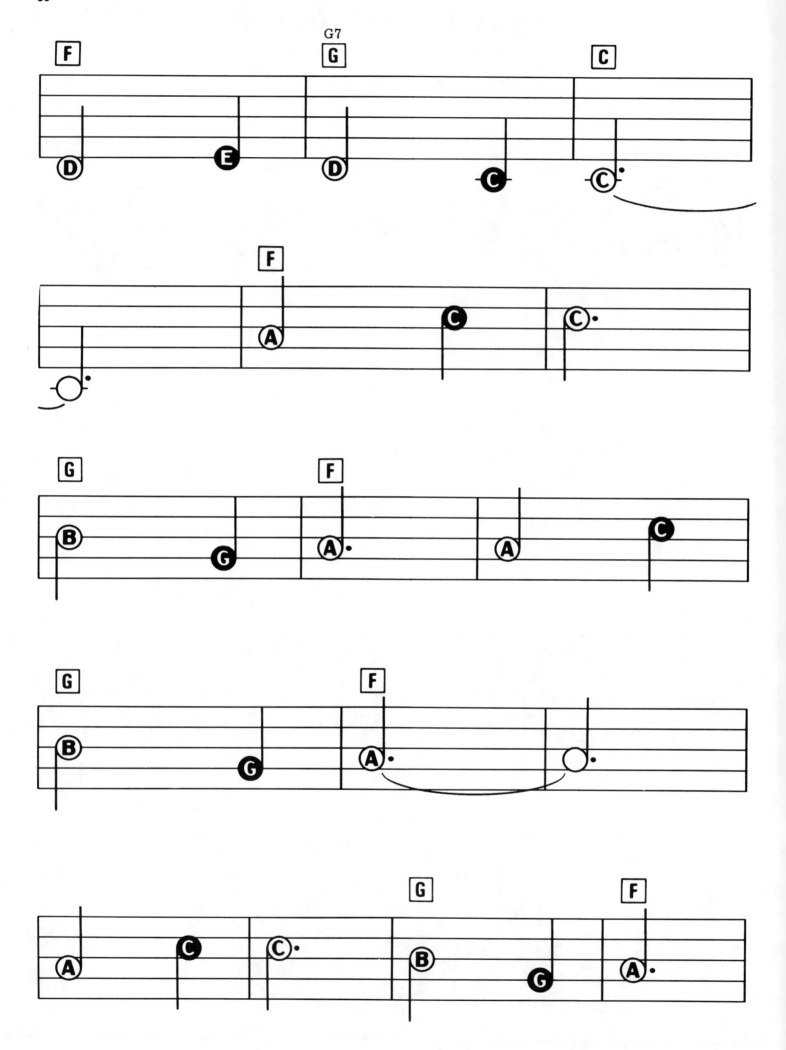

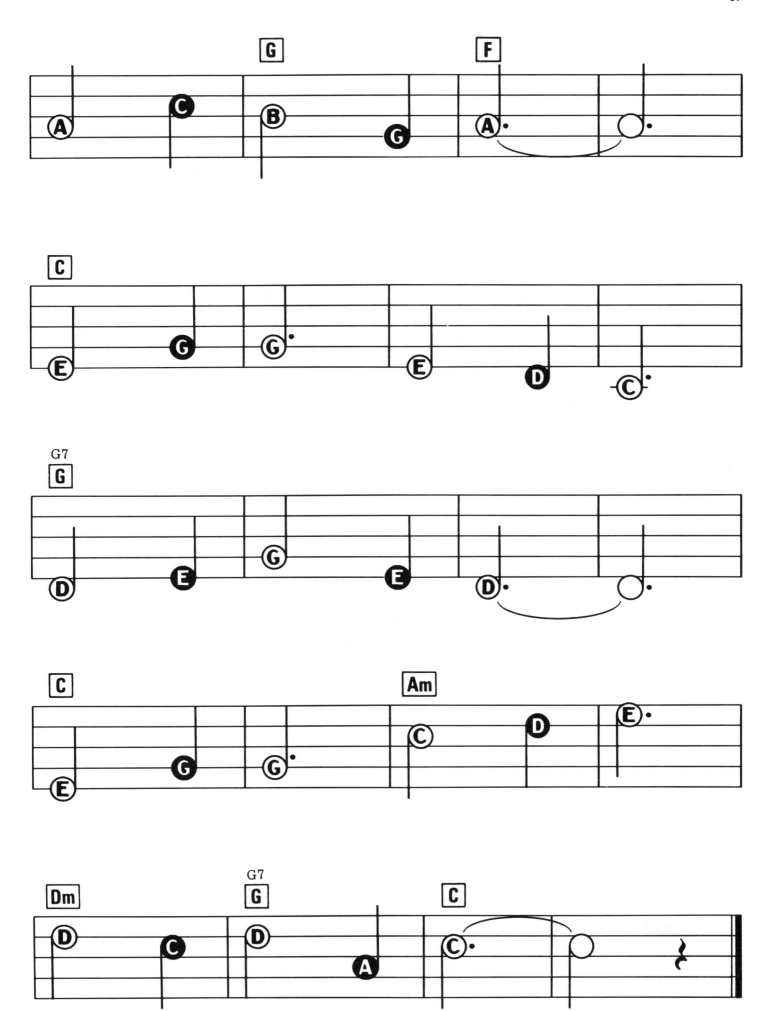

Symphony No. 9
(Fourth Movement Theme, "Ode To Joy")

Registration 5
Rhythm: March

Ludwig van Beethoven

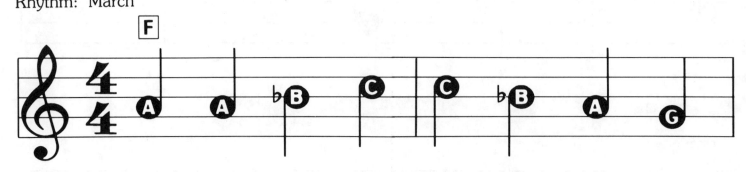

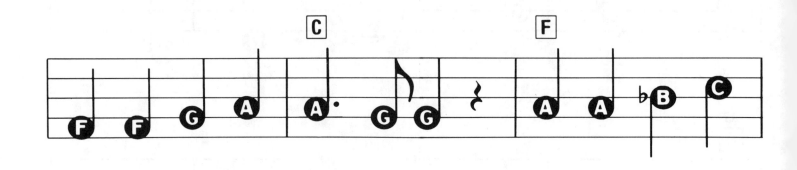

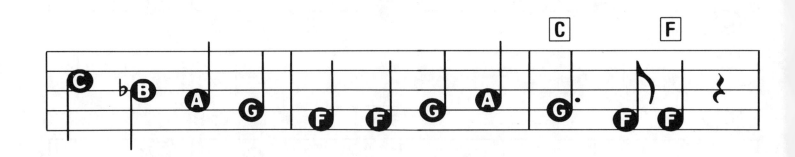

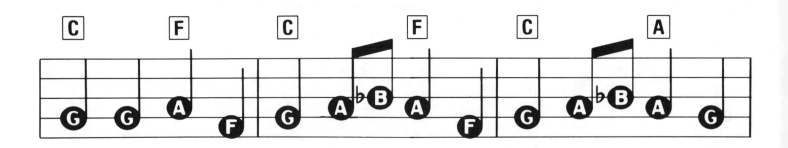

Copyright © 1992 by HAL LEONARD PUBLISHING CORPORATION
International Copyright Secured   All Rights Reserved

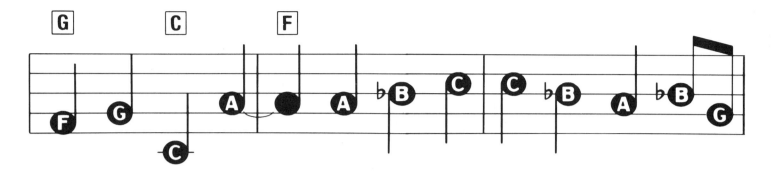
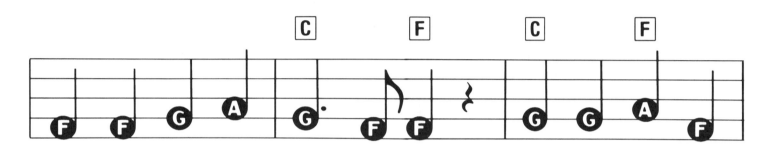
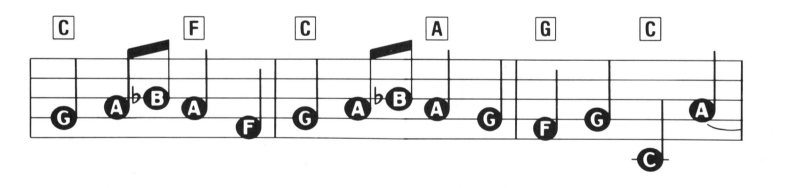
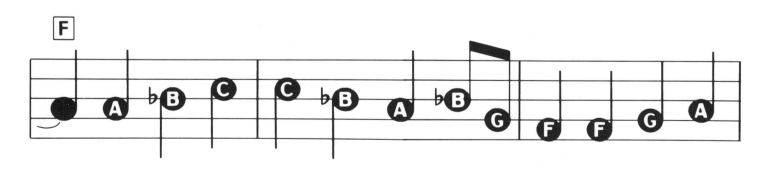

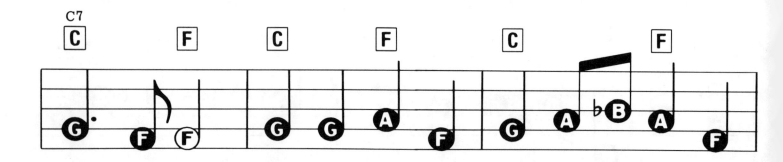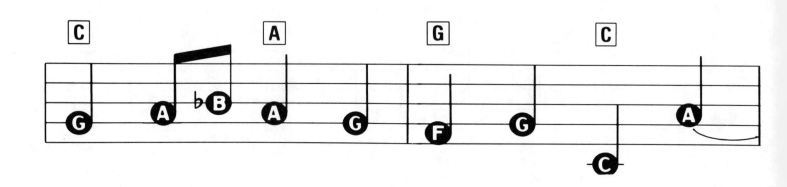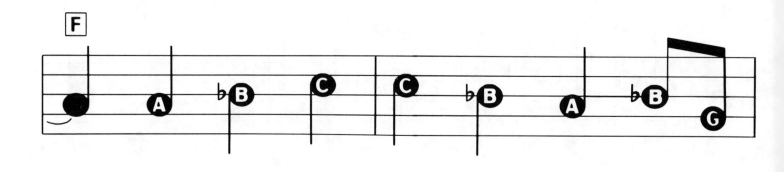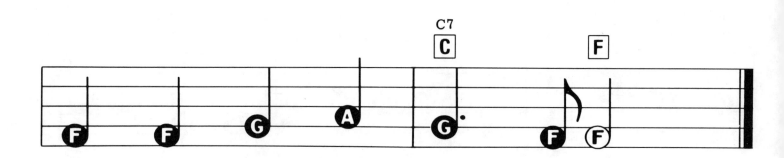

Symphony No. 40
(First Movement Theme)

Registration 3
Rhythm: 8 Beat or Rock (Optional)

Wolfgang Amadeus Mozart

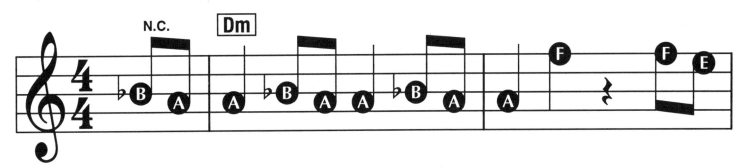
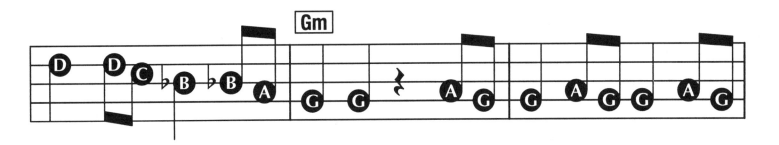
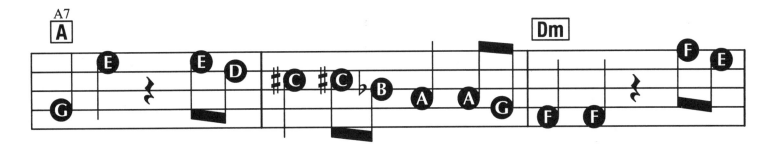
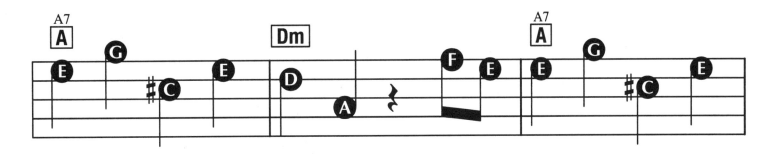
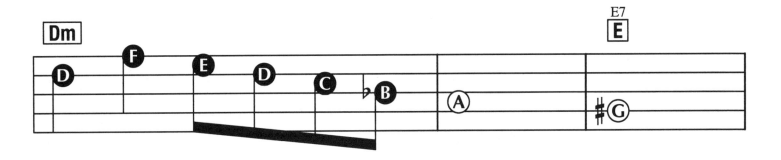

Copyright © 1992 by HAL LEONARD PUBLISHING CORPORATION
International Copyright Secured   All Rights Reserved

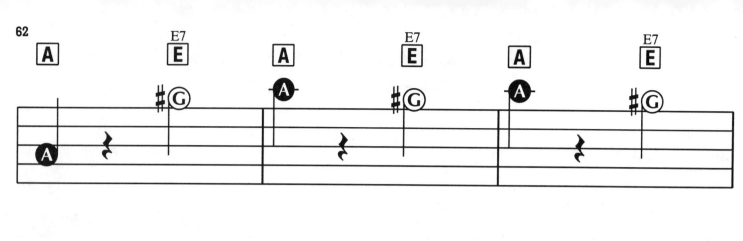
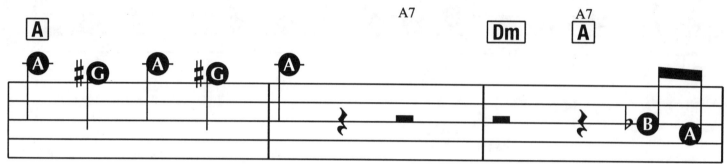
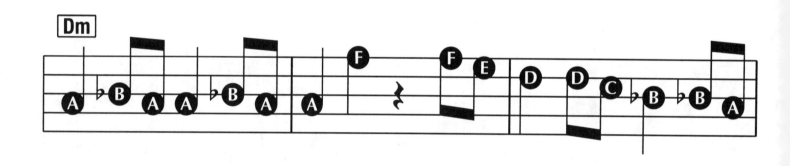
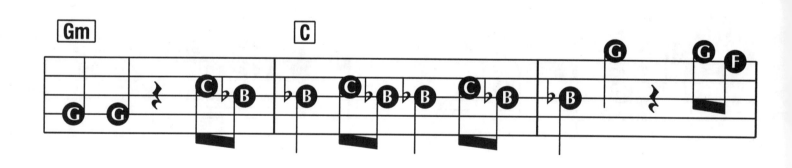
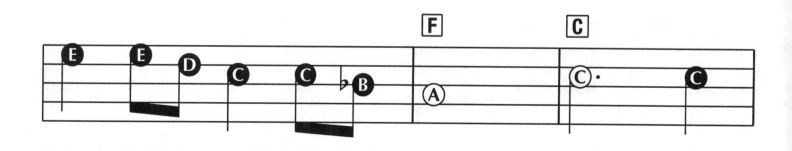

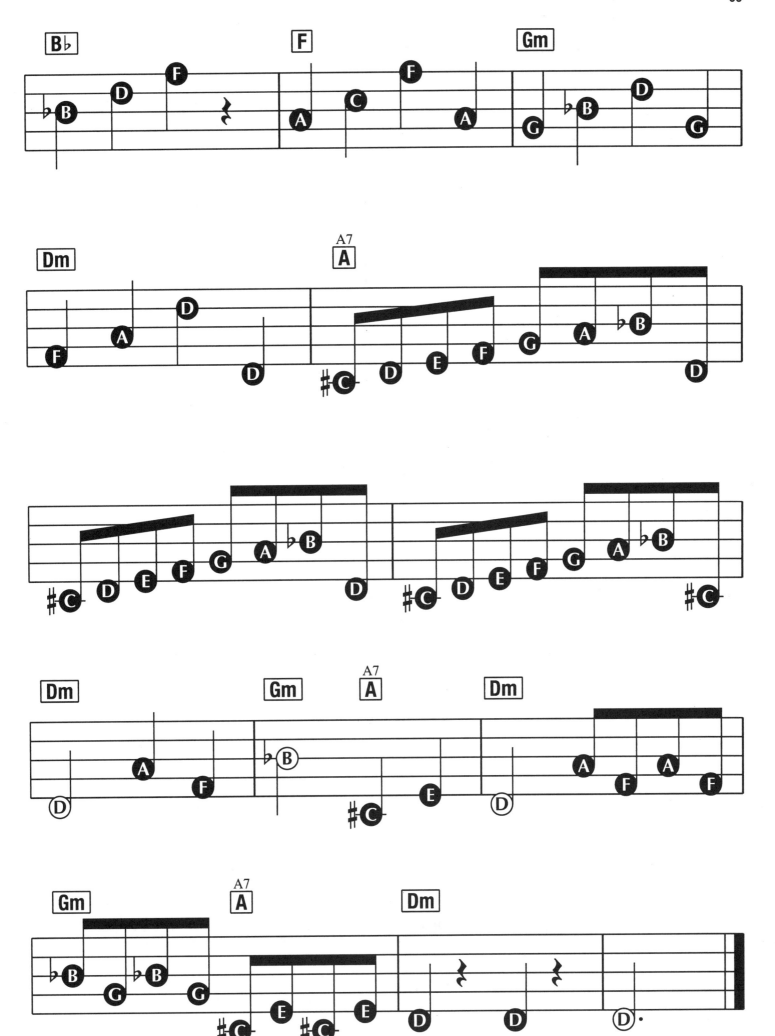

Violin Concerto
(First Movement Theme)

Registration 6
Rhythm: Disco

Felix Mendelssohn

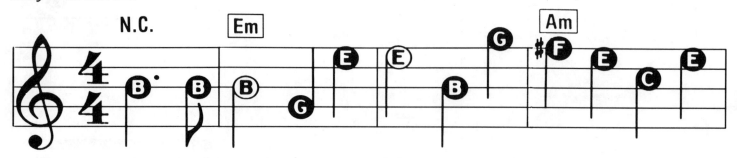
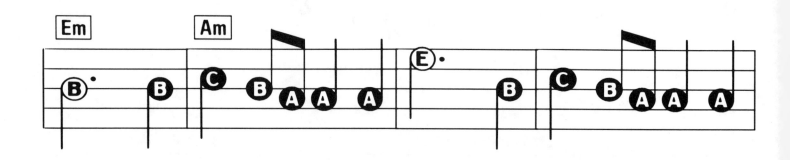
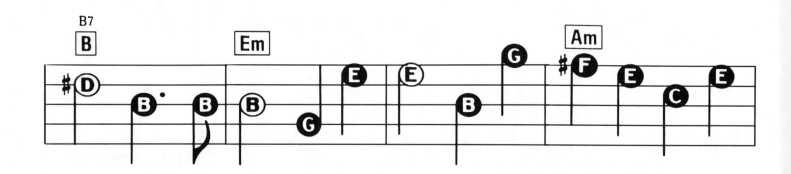
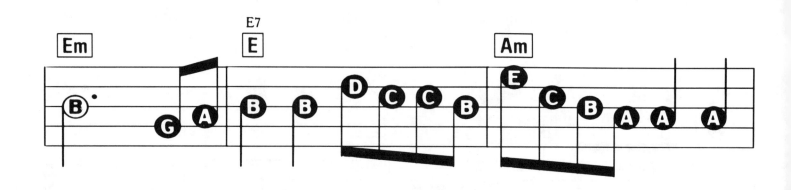

Copyright © 1992 by HAL LEONARD PUBLISHING CORPORATION
International Copyright Secured   All Rights Reserved

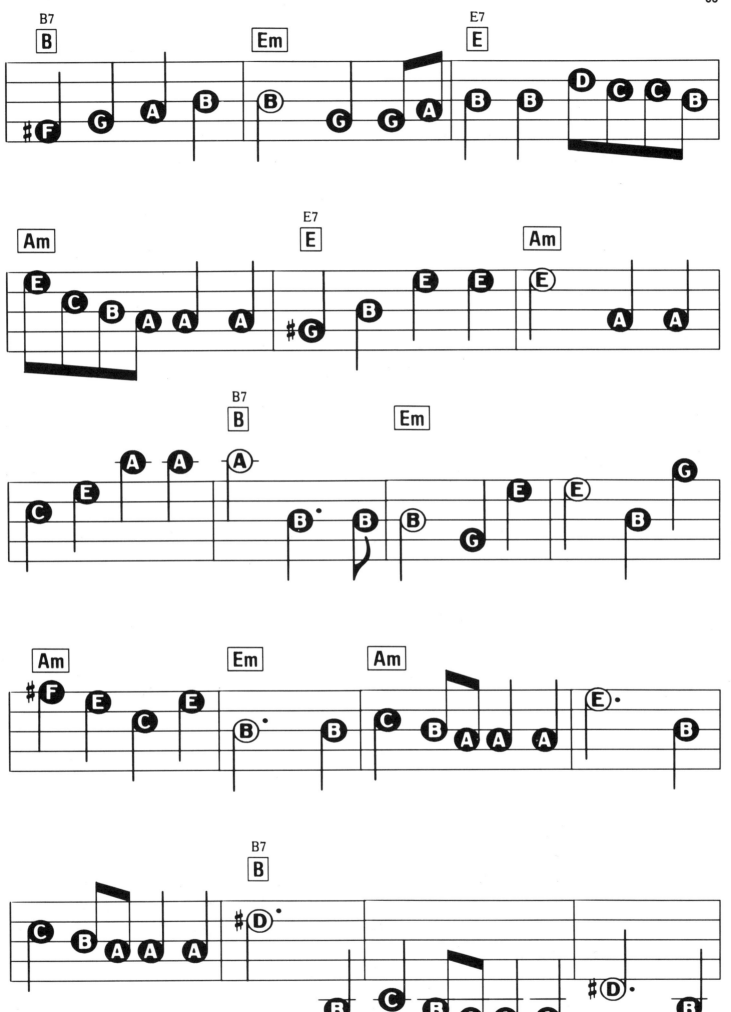

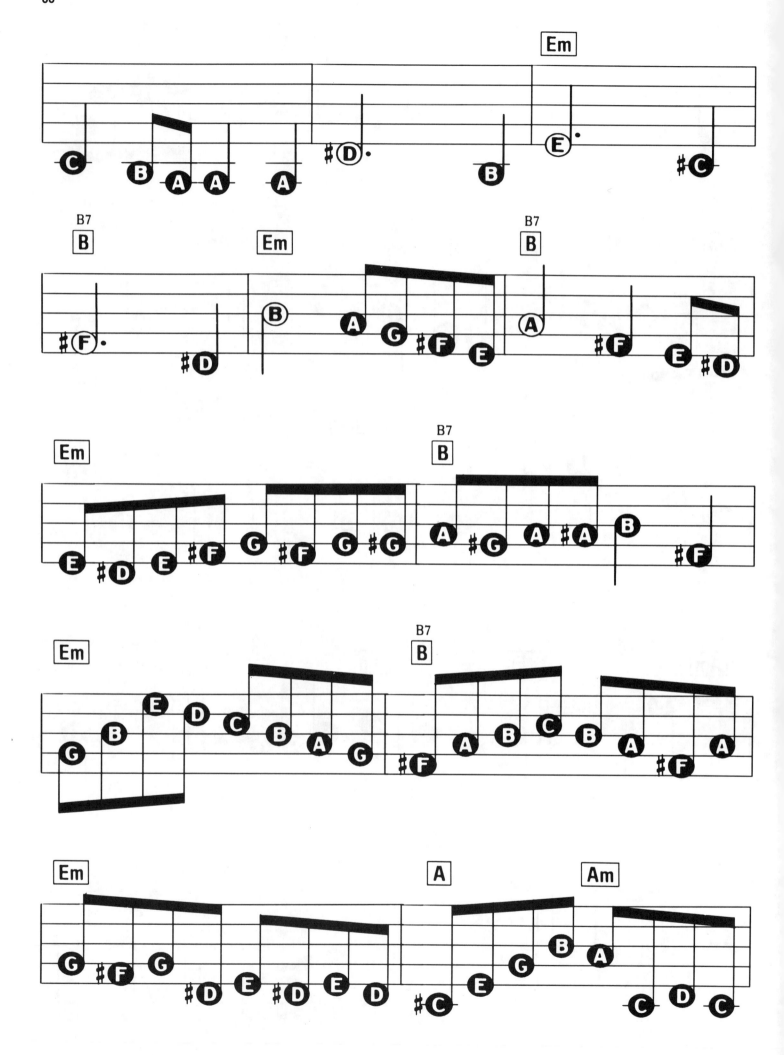

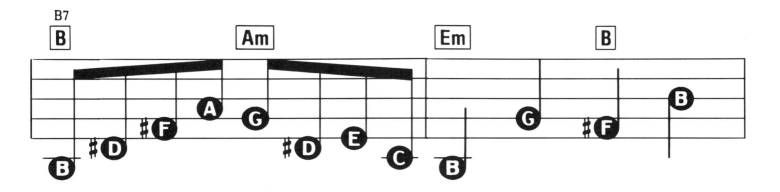
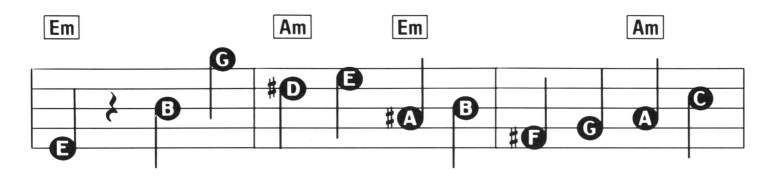
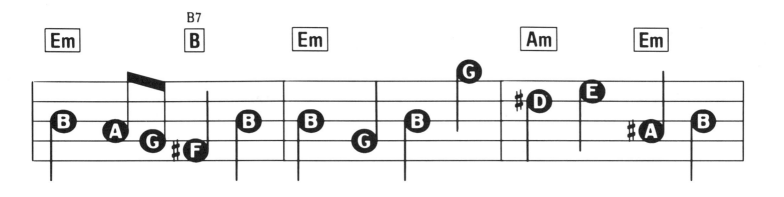
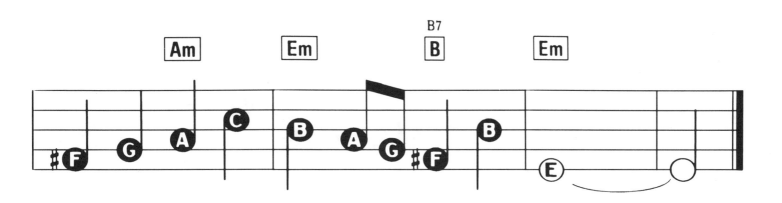

William Tell Overture
(Closing Theme)

Registration 7
Rhythm: March

Gioachino Rossini

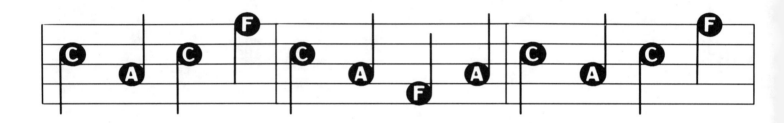
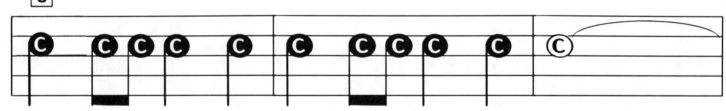
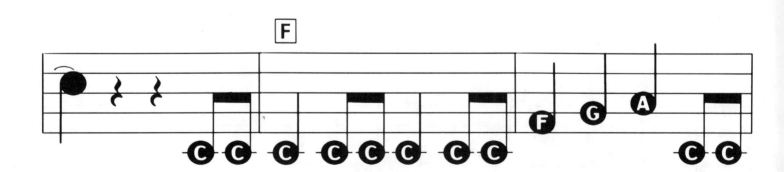

Copyright © 1992 by HAL LEONARD PUBLISHING CORPORATION
International Copyright Secured   All Rights Reserved

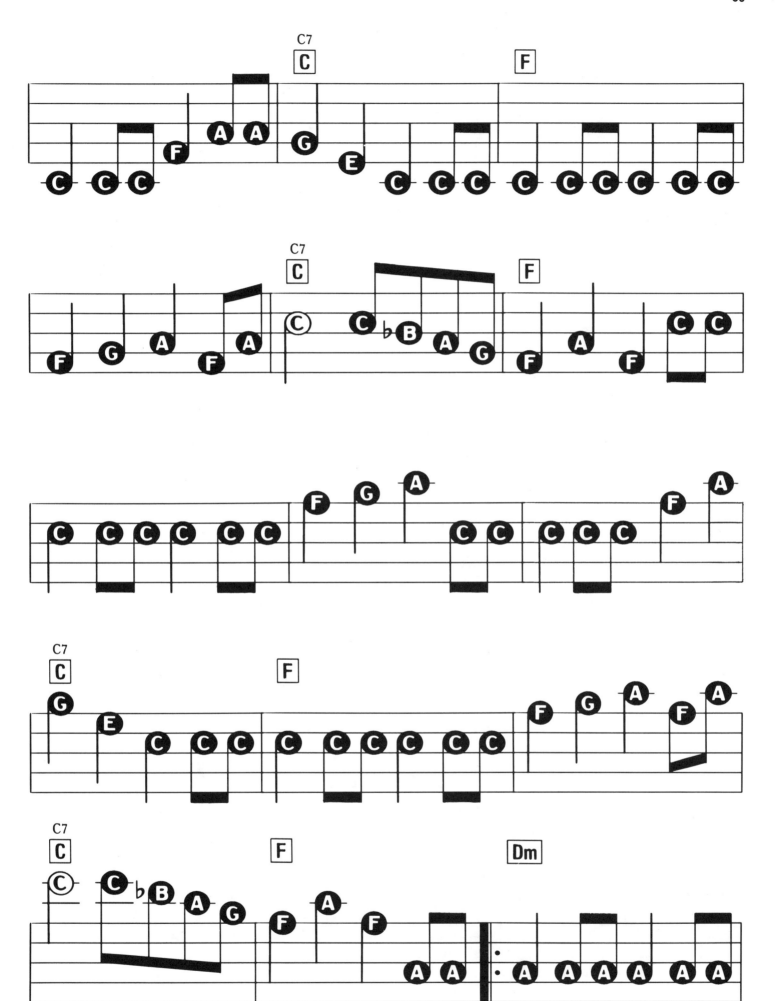

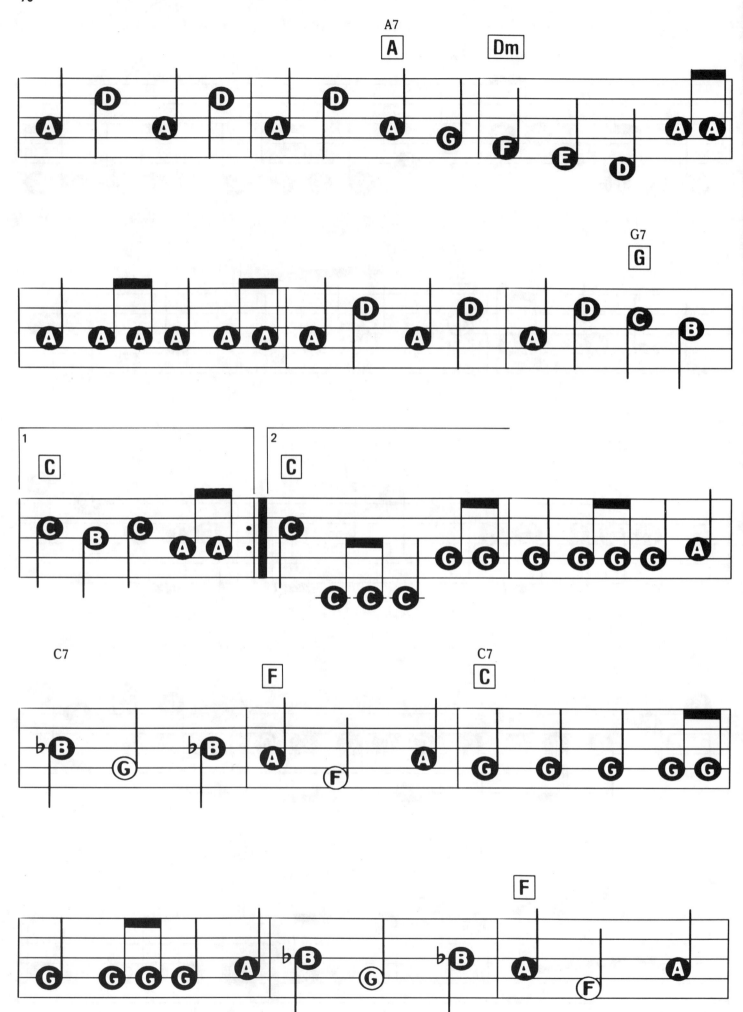

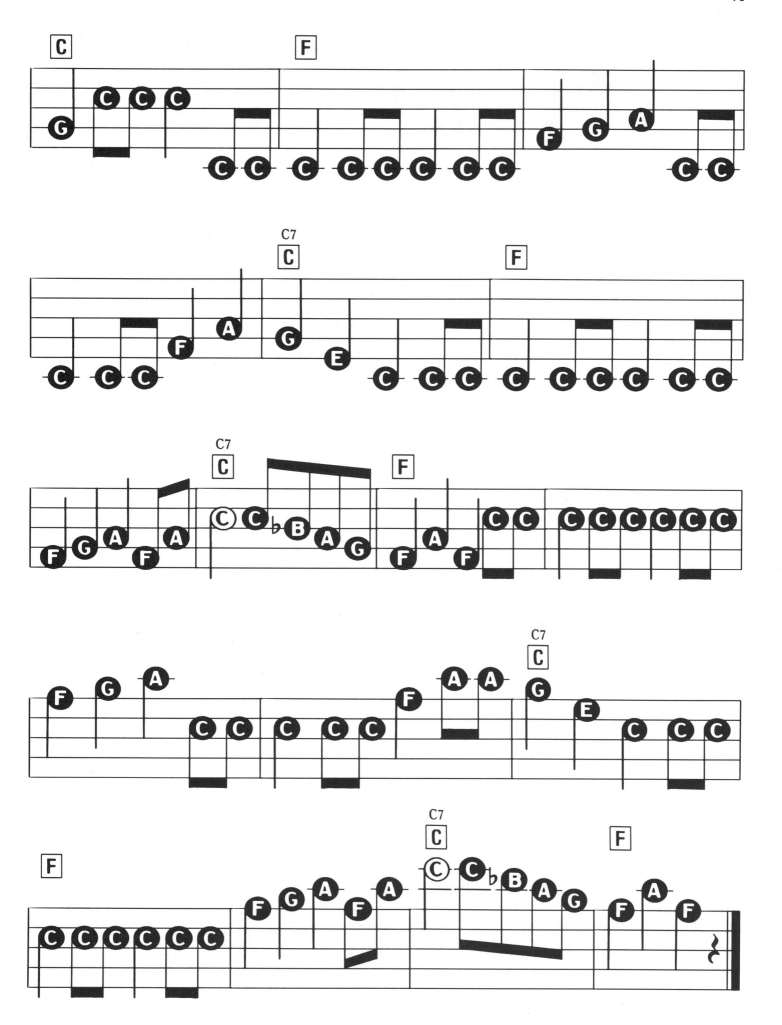

Registration Guide

- Match the Registration number on the song to the corresponding numbered category below. Select and activate an instrumental sound available on your instrument.
- Choose an automatic rhythm appropriate to the mood and style of the song. (Consult your Owner's Guide for proper operation of automatic rhythm features.)
- Adjust the tempo and volume controls to comfortable settings.

Registration

1	Flute, Pan Flute, Jazz Flute
2	Clarinet, Organ
3	Violin, Strings
4	Brass, Trumpet
5	Synth Ensemble, Accordion, Brass
6	Pipe Organ, Harpsichord
7	Jazz Organ, Vibraphone, Vibes, Electric Piano, Jazz Guitar
8	Piano, Electric Piano
9	Trumpet, Trombone, Clarinet, Saxophone, Oboe
10	Violin, Cello, Strings